W9-CJN-188

144.3
W72f

63971

DATE DUE			
GAYLORD M-2			PRINTED IN U.S.A.

WITHDRAWN

Studies in Educational Theory
of the John Dewey Society   **NUMBER 5**

F. C. S. Schiller and the Dimensions of Pragmatism

The Commission on Studies in Educational Theory
Appointed by The John Dewey Society

Frederick Ellis
Western Washington State College

Ward Madden
Brooklyn College,
The City University of New York

Israel Scheffler
Harvard University

Robert Mason, Chairman
University of Pittsburgh

F. C. S. Schiller and the Dimensions
of Pragmatism

by **KENNETH WINETROUT**

CARL A. RUDISILL LIBRARY
LENOIR RHYNE COLLEGE

OHIO STATE UNIVERSITY PRESS

144.3
W 72f

63971

December, 1968

Copyright © 1967 by the Ohio State University Press
All Rights Reserved
Library of Congress Catalogue Card Number: 67–22738

Foreword

Many observers of the contemporary philosophical scene are perturbed by the way in which it has been split into two—not into two opposing factions or camps, but into two arenas. There is the one group of philosophers (largely Anglo-American, Scandinavian, and former Viennese) who are concerned with logical analysis, conceptual elucidation, positivism, science, empiricism, and problems of language; they can be conveniently encapsulated as the analytic philosophers. The other group (largely French and German) deal with metaphysics, religion, philosophical anthropology, and phenomenology; they can be found under that capacious umbrella called existentialism. The first group tries hard to introduce precision and clarity into carefully delineated problems of philosophy; its achievements have been in such areas as the structure of science, the concept of necessary truth, the foundations of mathematics, the nature of logic, the relation of meaning to language, the dependence of ethics on the social and biological sciences, the inquiry into sense perception, and many others. The existentialists, on the other hand, are passionately involved in large and ultimate questions centering on the place of man in the universe, on freedom and destiny, on commitment, on God, and on death. The great names in the analytic movement are Russell, Moore, Wittgenstein, and Carnap; among the existentialists, Kierkegaard, Heidegger, Husserl, and Sartre.

But neither group ever talks to the other. Neither thinks the other is "doing philosophy." The analysts regard existententialism as fuzzy, murky, confused, and adolescent. The existentialists think analytic philosophy is trivial, pedantic, pedestrian, and neo-scholastic.

It is the great insight of Kenneth Winetrout's position that pragmatism can be the bridge between the two groups. He sees pragmatism as containing the seeds of both points of view; analytic precision in Peirce, existentialist concern with the human situation in James and Schiller, and both in Dewey. The verifiability theory of meaning, for example, which has been a linchpin of analytic philosophy, may legitimately be found foreshadowed in the instrumental or pragmatic theory of meaning and truth. And the existentialist stress on freedom and choice, on a man-centered ontology, may be seen quite clearly in Schiller's and James's humanism.

Dr. Winetrout views pragmatism as the legitimate philosophical outcome of many currents in American intellectual life, such as cultural pluralism, a high regard for the achievements of science, economic and political reform, religious ferment, personalism, subjectivism, and a concern for social improvement.

Although Dr. Winetrout believes that pragmatism represented a high-water mark in American philosophy, he thinks it no longer occupies that eminence; rather, he speaks of its "death." May I not suggest, however, that a better reason may be given for the fact that "pragmatic philosophy" is seldom explicitly advocated today? Has it not become part of the intellectual air we breathe? Is it not a residue in our thought that we take for granted? In Plato's *Protagoras,* Socrates has asked who it is who teaches men how to be good. "All men are teachers of virtue," answers Protagoras, "each one according to his ability; and you say, Where are the teachers? You might as well ask, Who teaches Greek? For of that too there will not be any teachers found." No one today has to teach us pragmatism as such.

Perhaps uniquely among philosophical movements, pragmatism has been a philosophy not only for the academy and the cloister but for the whole gamut of human problems. Dr. Winetrout shows us how it has impinged upon, and influenced, politics, education, law, psychology, religion, and social activity. Philosophy for the pragmatists is not an activity distinct from human culture; rather, like literature, religion, art, science, ethics, and social policy, it is a part of it. Philosophy, as Dewey put it, should be concerned not only with the problems of philosophers but also with the problems of men.

Schiller occupies the center of Dr. Winetrout's stage, and his contributions are sympathetically evaluated. But James, Peirce, and Dewey are discussed thoroughly, and the interrelations of their doctrines are clarified. Philosophy was very exciting when they trod the earth. Even their errors were worth making. Schiller and Dewey were, in different ways, critics of traditional formal logic. As matters worked out, their views have not secured general acceptance by logicians today. But how breathtaking were their attempts!

A good deal of the vigor and daring of pragmatism comes through vividly in Dr. Winetrout's book. It is a valuable conspectus both of what makes pragmatism the distinctive philosophical achievement of modern America and of the important sense in which pragmatism is the progenitor of philosophical analysis and existentialism.

REUBEN ABEL

Graduate Faculty
New School for Social Research

Acknowledgments

The author—with a frank avowal of nostalgia for the 1930's, the issues and the personalities of that decade—wants to say a tender word of thanks to the memory of Boyd H. Bode, Joseph K. Hart, and H. Gordon Hullfish, who introduced him to pragmatism on hot summer days at the Ohio State University. There was one particularly hot day. Boyd Bode was climbing the steps to Arps Hall after meeting with one of his large classes. He turned, with a gesture to the heat and humidity, and said to a number of students, "I guess I'll just have to let the world save itself." In a spirit of humility, not of arrogance, these men did feel that they had a part to play in saving the world.

For encouragement to pursue this work on Schiller, the exiled pragmatist, warm thanks are given to Reuben Abel of the New School, Gail Kennedy of Amherst College, Israel Scheffler of Harvard University, and Arthur Wirth of Washington University. The author is also grateful to Robert E. Mason and the members of his Commission for their help and suggestions. A cordial word of thanks goes to Robert S. Demorest, of the Ohio

State University Press, for his editorial assistance. Evelyn Jackson, librarian at the American International College, was generous with her time in securing Schiller's books from various university libraries. And to Judy, Mark, and Nancy: thanks for being so considerate.

KENNETH WINETROUT

Hampden, Massachusetts

Table of Contents

F. C. S. Schiller and the Dimensions of Pragmatism

I. Introduction

That particular hour when there is much talk about the death of a movement may be the very time to examine the birth of the movement. An exercise in last rites should in all fairness make some reference to beginnings.

In recent years we have heard a good deal about the death of pragmatism. Some mourners have stopped short of obituaries and have merely put pragmatism on the critical list. Morton White wrote:

> Abroad books were destroyed; here they glided out of public view. I have in mind the submersion of a certain style of thinking which dominated America for almost half a century—an intellectual pattern compounded of pragmatism, institutionalism, behaviorism, legal realism, economic determinism, the "new history." When we consider the illustrious names in these traditions we become even more aware of the end of an era—John Dewey, Thorstein Veblen, Justice Holmes, Charles A. Beard, James Harvey Robinson.

It might be argued that these movements are not dead,

but one cannot avoid feeling that they are past the peak of their influence. These are days in which Dewey's views are being replaced by Kierkegaard's in places where once Dewey was king. . . .

Some may deny that the demise or the decline is connected with the war and the atomic era. Maybe not. But surely it took place in the popular mind sometime during the ten years before we were engulfed by war, and most likely the decline was connected with the forces that overwhelmed us.[1]

White used 1930 as a dividing line. "By 1930 a line had been broken, and the remaining soldiers marched in different directions and enlisted in new regiments." [2] When some eight years later, in 1957, a new edition of his book appeared, White noted that what he had seen as "the declining reputation of certain American liberal thinkers" had grown into "a powerful effort to discredit the ideas and outlook of some of the most distinguished Americans of the twentieth century." [3] Charles Frankel has taken the position that "pragmatism was the most important philosophy of the 'golden age.'" [4] By golden age, he referred to the period from 1870 to 1930. John E. Smith, in a review of philosophic thought in the United States, asserted that pragmatism had been unable to sustain itself as a major outlook among academic philosophers.[5] Brand Blanshard has viewed the philosophy of analysis as dominating almost all important university posts in the United States.[6]

Lawrence Cremin [7] found it quite appropriate to have a double ceremony and placed progressive education in a common grave with pragmatism. Kimball and McClellan spoke of the "denigration, if not the abandonment of a philosophic position which had provided the basic ideology of the educational profession for so many decades." [8] Further, we have read

of "the-going-out-of-fashion of both pragmatism and progressiv-
ism," and there has been mention of a "posthumous garland." [9]
Paul Nash,[10] disturbed by all this talk, went looking for the
body of progressive education and professed that he could not
find it. But body or no body, a funeral air has settled over both
pragmatism and progressive education for a number of
years—or as some would have it, for several decades.

We do not turn to birth as a kind of reassuring antidote to
death; rather, we look into origins as a way of determining
whether the corpse we are about to lower into the grave is
correctly identified as well as wholly dead. Too often, in our
haste, we bury prematurely. Too often we falsify the papers
and bury a corpse under an assumed name.

We may think of this book as a cautionary statement. It
proposes to examine the origins of pragmatism in order to
qualify the death notices, or possibly to contradict them. An
exploration of origins may take various forms. It may focus
upon the primary figure in a movement. For pragmatism, there
can be little doubt that the key name is John Dewey. Another
approach may concentrate on the impact a movement has had
on central disciplines; this would study such questions as what
effect pragmatism has had on logic, political science, psychology, and so on. There is also what we may call the historical
method, which seeks the place of the particular topic in the
large sweep of history.

This book uses another perspective. It looks at a man who is
seen on the contemporary philosophic stage but dimly, as a
minor figure in pragmatism: Ferdinand Canning Scott Schiller
(1864–1937). But Schiller was not always a minor figure in
pragmatism. In the pristine days of pragmatism, Schiller was a
major figure. As a formulator, as a propagator, in the annals of
the inception of pragmatism, Schiller must be placed as a peer
of Peirce, James, Dewey, and Mead.

In the 1950's and 60's, Schiller seems virtually forgotten, and is scarcely read or mentioned. A paper read by this author in honor of Schiller's centennial year went so far as to suggest that maybe we should forget all about him. The paper posited that the world is so full of a number of things, we should all be wary of adding to that number of things. And so when a man's centennial year arrives, one asks whether we should pronounce a second ceremony of final rites or should use the occasion to raise the banner of a revival. Ferdinand Canning Scott Schiller is a test case. Any careful survey of philosophy in the 1960's will indicate that Schiller has been put out of mind. Some scholars come to their centennial year still so vividly in public consciousness that the world has to be informed that they have died, whereas others approach their centennial year so vaguely existent in footnotes that the world has to be informed that they have lived. Schiller belongs to this second category. Are we so busy with the philosophical things of the 1960's that we should not reintroduce Schiller into the philosophical stream?

Perhaps it will be granted that the structuring of a review of origins around a relatively unknown man has certain advantages. For one thing, it adds a certain freshness; we are not going over well-trodden ground. There is a good possibility that this procedure will act as a wide-angle lens to our viewpoint. Then, of course, it could even happen that the man who got left out may, when reintroduced, prove extremely relevant to the contemporary scene. The world is by no means so simple that a major or minor figure forever possesses the same proportionate relevance to each succeeding era. Major and minor roles may be exchanged as we advance from period to period.

Since Schiller has been so little in the philosophic news since his death in 1937, a few words about his life and work seem necessary. Reuben Abel's *The Pragmatic Humanism of F.*

C. S. Schiller, 1955,[11] is the lone book on Schiller. This book examines Schiller's philosophy in a sympathetic manner and includes an extensive bibliography of books and articles by Schiller. Fourteen books and more than one hundred articles and book reviews are listed. "In the years in which Schiller and his ideas were a _cause célèbre,_ the magazine articles flew thick and fast," wrote Abel. "Schiller was himself a vigorous and prolific polemicist. . . . Usually he left no stone unturned or unflung in chiding his adversaries." [12]

Schiller's major books are: _Riddles of the Sphinx,_ 1891; _Humanism,_ 1903; _Studies in Humanism,_ 1907; _Formal Logic,_ 1912; _Logic for Use,_ 1929; _Must Philosophers Disagree?,_ 1934; and _Our Human Truths,_ 1937. In addition to these, there are books on politics and eugenics. One essay, "Axioms as Postulates," must be regarded as a major contribution.

Schiller was educated at Rugby and Oxford. He taught German briefly at Eton, then returned to Oxford to teach. He was at Cornell University from 1893 to 1897. While at Cornell, he failed the doctorate oral in philosophy. He went back to Oxford in 1897 and taught there until 1926. Between 1926 and 1935 he spent part of each academic year at the University of Southern California and at Oxford. From 1935 until his death, August 9, 1937, he made California his permanent home.

Schiller was a true cosmopolite. He was born in Denmark of a German father whose income came from commercial enterprises in India, and who sent his sons to England for their education. During most of Schiller's life his family had a villa in Switzerland. There he spent his summers hiking and swimming and playing host to many of his students as well as to some of the world's famous people.

Of all the early pragmatists, Schiller had the least to say

about education; what little he did say was more often amusing than profound. He did his "educational work" as an exemplar of the good teacher. One of his students commented thus:

> I am delighted to have a chance of saying how much I owe to Schiller as a tutor. It is no exaggeration to say that I am more grateful to him than to any of the people to whom I brought essays. He took immense pains over his pupils, and, as a tutor, displayed nothing of that rather facetious cleverness which irritated a good many people. He would never evade difficulties you might put to him—in fact, he encouraged you to state any difficulties you had, and never tried to "come it over you." I must have been considerable trial to him because I had no special bent for philosophy, and yet I was both argumentative and desperately sincere about it all. It would have hurt my feelings very much indeed if I had thought either that Schiller was not troubling to answer my arguments, or that he wasn't as anxious as I was to find out what things meant. Undergraduates are very quick to notice any indifference or flippancy of this kind in their tutors, and I never had the least feeling that I was being played with. . . . I was also most grateful to Schiller for his general kindness. He was most hospitable to his pupils. He used to ask them to breakfast when he had people staying with him whom he thought they would like to meet. I remember meeting Bergson, Lowes Dickinson, H. G. Wells, in this way. . . . I never once heard Schiller try to evade a question, or to give the kind of clever, unconvincing answer which a don can always give to an undergraduate's questions if he wants to burke the issue.[13]

The one thing on which every one seems in agreement regarding Schiller is that he was a first-class wit—in small talk on hikes, in classroom lectures, and in philosophic talk of the highest order. One of his last essays carries the title, "Must Philosophy be Dull?" He himself could see no reason why in the nature of things philosophy had to be dull. He said, "I do not recognize the duty of dullness, and I am even sceptical of the dullness of duty." [14]

But academic philosophy turns out quite often to be quite dull. He pointed out:

> It conscientiously rehearses all the errors into which speculative philosophy has fallen in the past when it had not sufficient means to solve its problems. The more pedestrian of philosophers wander about in them with their heads in *culs de sac;* the more dashing pursue dead issues into dead ends. . . . Hence they leave behind them litter, but not literature.
>
> There are also other reasons why academic philosophy should be dull. It is often considered essential that academic philosophy should not arouse and inflame the minds of the young: it should be "safe" and dull men are safe. . . . However, the desire for safety and the routine of instruction are far less potent generators of dullness than is the desire to impress each other which fills the souls of pedants. These also play for safety, and find that it is most easily attained by obscurity, technicality and the invention of a new terminology, for what one cannot be sure he understands he cannot confute and does not dare criticize. . . . It is sometimes quite amusing to watch an encounter between two such grandees of the learned world. They take their stand firmly on their dignity and never emerge from the protective shadow of their "systems." Each speaks pontifically in his own language, each probably in jargon which pretty perfectly conforms to the German wit's definition of philosophy as "nothing but the systematic misuse of a terminology invented expressly for this purpose." . . . So they never understand each other,

and they rarely even try to do so. They just gibber at each other! [15]

His conclusion: "Philosophy may be dull; but it need not be dull unless philosophers prefer to have it so and make it so." [16]

John Passmore identified Schiller's style as an integral part of his protest when he wrote: "Himself an Oxford man, he was in revolt against the smugness and rigidity which . . . Oxford encouraged and even extolled. His very style was a protest." [17] Ralph Tyler Flewelling had Schiller in mind when he made this comment: "But while humor is the balance-wheel of sound thinking, it is too rare in the seats of philosophy. It is a bird that should be found in every campus tree but has seldom been known to light there and is never encouraged." [18] The University of Southern California at least enjoyed the presence of Schiller for some years.

Abel concluded his centennial tribute with: "Anglo-American philosophy is much more precise today than when Schiller flourished; but it is not nearly so lively." [19]

This, then, is the man whom this book proposes to reintroduce into philosophic discussion as a function of reviewing the origins of pragmatism and of identifying certain dimensions in pragmatism from its beginning in the last decades of the nineteenth century through the first several decades of the twentieth century. From the present vantage point and in the current vocabulary, we may think of pragmatism as having three initial thrusts: Charles S. Peirce represents the analytical thrust; John Dewey, the reformist thrust; and William James and F. C. S. Schiller, the existentialist thrust. It is when we are unmindful of what pragmatism was in its beginnings that we find it inadequate in our own time. The hope that inspires this book is that a review of Schiller may show, in one way, the timeliness of pragmatism for contemporary philosophy and philosophy of education.

1. Morton White, *Social Thought in America* (1957 ed.; Boston: Beacon Press), pp. 3–4.

2. *Ibid.*, p. 10.

3. *Ibid.*, p. ix.

4. Charles Frankel (ed.), *The Golden Age of American Philosophy* (New York: George Braziller, 1960), p. 13.

5. John E. Smith, *The Spirit of American Philosophy* (New York: Oxford University Press, 1963), p. 198.

6. Brand Blanshard, "The Changing Climate in Philosophy," *Liberal Education,* May, 1961, p. 230.

7. Lawrence A. Cremin, *The Transformation of the School* (New York: Alfred Knopf, 1961).

8. Solon T. Kimball and James E. McClellan, *Education and the New America* (New York: Random House, 1962), p. 88.

9. *Ibid.*, pp. 110–11.

10. Paul Nash, "The Strange Death of Progressive Education," *Educational Theory,* April, 1964.

11. Reuben Abel, *The Pragmatic Humanism of F. C. S. Schiller* (New York: King's Crown Press, 1955). Dr. Abel has also edited a book of selections from the early works of Schiller, *Humanistic Pragmatism* (New York: Free Press, 1966).

12. Abel, *The Pragmatic Humanism of F. C. S. Schiller*, p. 179.

13. E. L. Woodward in R. R. Marett, "Ferdinand Canning Scott Schiller, 1864–1937," *Proceedings of the British Academy*, XXIII, 8–9.

14. F. C. S. Schiller, *Our Human Truths* (New York: Columbia University Press, 1939), p. 93.

15. *Ibid.*, pp. 100–101.

16. *Ibid.*, p. 102.

17. John Passmore, *A Hundred Years of Philosophy* (London: Gerald Duckworth & Co., 1957), p. 115.

18. Ralph Tyler Flewelling, "F. C. S. Schiller, an Appreciation," *The Personalist,* January, 1938, p. 7.

19. Reuben Abel, "F. C. S. Schiller and Pragmatism," *The Personalist,* Summer, 1964, p. 324.

II. James and Schiller: The Pristine Days of Pragmatism

We have it from no less an authority than John Dewey that pragmatism originated with Charles Sanders Peirce (1839–1914). Dewey declared: "The origin of Pragmatism goes back to Charles Sanders Peirce, the son of one of the most celebrated mathematicians of the United States, and himself very proficient in the science of mathematics; he is one of the founders of the modern symbolic logic of relations." [1] Rarely in the history of philosophy has the birth of a movement been so carefully pinpointed: one man, Peirce; one essay, "How to Make Our Ideas Clear," published in 1878; and one passage in that essay: "Consider what effects, which might conceivably have practical bearings, we conceive the object of our conception to have. Then, our conception of these effects is the whole of our conception of the object." [2]

This is scarcely the easiest prose with which to begin a major philosophical movement. W. B. Gallie offered some explanation for the turn of phrasings in this historical statement, when he wrote:

. . . We shall find good grounds for maintaining that, despite its verbal clumsiness—its heavy reiteration of the words "conception," "conceivable," "conceive," and its abrupt introduction of the phrase "practical bearings"—this maxim was formulated with great care; only—and this is all too typical of its author—his efforts were directed at bringing out the essentials of his own thought rather than at introducing the idea Pragmatism, helpfully if somewhat superficially, to the general reader.[3]

Gallie went on to say that Peirce had given in 1871 a "rough adumbration" of the 1878 statement. The earlier formulation is not one bit easier to read, but it gives every indication of the direction of Peirce's thought.

A better rule for avoiding the deceits of language is this: Do things fulfil the same purpose practically? Then let them be distinguished. If I have learnt a formula in gibberish which in any way jogs my memory so as to enable me in each single case to act as though I had a general idea, what possible utility is there in distinguishing between such a gibberish formula and an idea? Why use the term a general idea in such a sense as to separate things which, for all experiential purposes, are the same? [4]

While there are some obvious parallels between the 1871 statement and the 1878 one, it is the 1878 comment that is almost universally accepted as the original proposition in pragmatism.

Whether as a result of the difficulty of the language, the obscurity of the author, or the temper of the times, not much happened for a few decades. It remained for William James to get pragmatism into the public eye. James tells us that Peirce's principle "lay entirely unnoticed by any one for twenty years," and then when he brought forward the term in 1898 at a speech in California, "times seemed ripe for its reception." [5] From 1898 to 1907 when James published his book *Pragmatism: A New Name for Some Old Ways of Thinking,* the word pragmatism spread. "On all hands we find the 'pragmatic movement' spoken of . . . ," James reported. "It is evident that the term applies itself conveniently to a number of tendencies that hitherto have lacked a collective name and it has come to stay." [6]

James may have rejoiced in all this newly won popularity, but not so Peirce. Even before James's book appeared, Peirce decided in 1905 to disengage himself from what he saw as the main stream of pragmatism. James was using the term for his special brand of radical empiricism. Furthermore, that "admirably clear and brilliant thinker, Mr. Ferdinand C. S. Schiller" had picked up the same name for what he had originally called "anthropomorphism." It was time, Peirce said, "to kiss his child good-bye and relinquish it to its higher destiny." Henceforth he would call his philosophy "pragmaticism," a term that he felt assured "was ugly enough to be safe from kidnappers." [7] As yet, no daring kidnapper has made his appearance.

Schiller made the following comment on Peirce's withdrawing action:

Its putative parent, Peirce, was so shocked by the fame of the doctrine fathered upon him, and so dismayed by the herculean exploits which it accomplished even in its cradle, that he was actually driven to disown his paternity, and to take refuge in a "pragmaticism" which he said, was ugly enough to be left severely alone. . . . Its real progenitor, James, could hardly restrain his nearest and dearest pupils from participating in the congenial labor of misrepresenting what they had never understood.[8]

Dewey commented that the pragmatism of Peirce "applies to a very narrow and limited universe of discourse." [9] There can be little doubt that the other founders of pragmatism had in mind something considerably more comprehensive than did Peirce.

Schiller referred to James as the "real progenitor" of pragmatism. If we think of the period from 1898, the year of James's California address, to 1910, the year of James's death, then Schiller's remark is accurate. However, it should be added that James had a great helpmate in Schiller during those years. But if we think of the period from 1916, the publication date of Dewey's *Democracy and Education,* to 1938, the publication date of his *Logic: The Theory of Inquiry,* then there can be no question but that Dewey is the "real progenitor." And if we should ask the progenitor question with specific regard for meaningfulness in the 1960's, we may have to conclude that Peirce is the "real progenitor."

If we were asked to name the leading representative of pragmatism, we would have to counter with another question: Which period of pragmatism is your concern? Nor would it be enough to inquire merely as to the period. An additional question may well be more important: Which thrust or emphasis of pragmatism is your concern?

It is the thesis of this book that when we look at the origins of pragmatism from the standpoint of the late 1960's, we see three related but withal clearly identifiable dimensions. Peirce represents the analytical dimension; James and Schiller, the existentialist; and Dewey, the social reformist. Others have separated these men in yet other ways. Bertrand Russell, for example, has called James the religious protagonist of pragmatism; Schiller, the literary; and Dewey, the scientific.[10] Gail Kennedy approached the problem from what were the primary concerns of these men before they became pragmatists.

Pierce had developed his pragmatism from studies of logic and scientific method under the influence of the scholastics and of Kant. James came to his formulation of pragmatism from the opposite direction, the study of psychology under the influence of the British empiricists and of Renouvier, and John Dewey arrived at his version of the doctrine—"instrumentalism" as he called it—from still a third starting point, that of neo-Hegelian idealism. . . . It is remarkable enough that, arising from such different backgrounds of interests and knowledge, their eventual positions so nearly converged; it is hardly surprising that they did not entirely coincide.[11]

Schiller seems to have come at pragmatism from an opposition to the idealism he found all around him at Oxford.

No categorization of men can be wholly fair, completely accurate. The scheme taken in this book, while in no way an attempt to achieve a neat pigeonholing, is offered as a heuristically useful device. When we deal with a man historically, we may find that which he became after his death quite as significant as what he did while alive. The reality of a man is not only in what he was; it may be quite as much in what he becomes.

A viability index on Peirce in the 1960's would point directly to his contribution as an analytic; and yet when he wrote, there was no school known as analysis. The same kind of an index applied to James, and Schiller would record them in the existentialist frame of reference; and again, there was no such school of philosophy under this title when they lived. The classification of Dewey is more complex because Dewey's total range of concern, of writing, was more inclusive than that of his fellows in the founding of pragmatism. Yet it does not seem particularly hazardous in the 1960's to hold that a viability index on Dewey would indicate that his reformist quality is at present the key inheritance from Dewey. The following opinion on John Dewey, while that of one man, may be much more commonly held than some persons would like to admit.

> There are fashions in philosophy as there are fashions in clothes, and John Dewey, like the long skirt, is no longer in fashion. People in education departments still fight about Dewey's philosophy of education, and neoconservatives like Kirk and Hallowell or Marxists like Selsam and Wells blame Dewey for most of the ills and muddles of our cultural and intellectual life, but, for the most part, Dewey and the philosophical approach he initiated have, temporarily at least, passed from the center of interest.
>
> True, Dewey has become an American institution. . . . But like Sinclair Lewis in literature, Dewey, in philosophy, no longer captures the imagination. . . .
>
> Philosophy for Dewey is concerned with social change and conflict. . . . Like Marx, Dewey did not only want to understand the world . . . he also wished to change it.[12]

To a man of Kai Nielsen's persuasion, Dewey is not a philosopher because in him the reformist quality is too central, too strong.

To push the thesis of this book yet another step: there is high coincidence between what we today in the late 1960's find *most alive* in Peirce, James, Dewey, or Schiller and what each of them *most stressed* when he was the "real progenitor" of pragmatism. Today we admire Peirce most for his analytical work; and surely, this is what most interested him during the height of his personal influence as a philosopher. Today we view James as the philosopher of the individual; and surely, this was his great message while still alive. Again, Dewey is not so easy; but those who read only what many think of today as Dewey's major philosophical works may never realize how much energy he devoted to reform causes. We get a better idea of this dimension in Dewey when we look at the essays in *Character and Events*.[13] For relevance to the present, the most viable part of Dewey seems actually to be his reformist quality.

A few pages ago a chronology of the very beginnings of pragmatism was presented. That history will be continued here by attempts to capture some of the spirit of that early period, as illustrated by exchanges between James and Schiller, and to show the existentialist tenor in both James and Schiller. While some persons may prefer to substitute "personalist" for "existentialist" in this context, the author finds "existentialist" to be as accurate and more appropriate for present purposes.

Schiller has not enjoyed a good press in the 1940's, 50's, and 60's. Indeed, one may say he has not even had a press at all. He is rarely mentioned in the history of philosophy texts. Passmore has given him about as much space as has any contemporary historian. When Schiller is called to the attention of readers, it is quite often as much with the intent of dismissing him as discussing him. For example, from Russell: "[In addition to James] there are two other protagonists of pragmatism, F. C. S. Schiller and John Dewey. I shall consider Dr. Dewey in the next chapter; Schiller was of less importance than the other two." [14] And this was Russell's total evaluation of Schiller in an eight-hundred-plus-page book on the history of philosophy in the West.

It is this sort of casual treatment that forces one to go into some detail to show how intimately Schiller was associated with James as a man and with pragmatism as a movement, and how in fact he was one of the founders of this movement.

James and Schiller met for the first time in the mid-1890's when Schiller spent some time in the James household during the Christmas holidays. James wrote a friend on this occasion: "I find him a peculiarly delightful fellow. His philosophy and mine run abreast in an altogether gratifying way to me." [15] Only three weeks before his death, James sent this last note of many he had sent to his younger friend Schiller: "I leave the cause in your hands. . . . Good-bye, and God bless you. . . . Keep your health, your splendid health. It is better than all the truths under the firmament. Ever thy W. J." [16]

Schiller responded with equal warmth to James, recording of their first encounter: "Five minutes after meeting him for the first time I found myself talking to him as if I had known him all my life. . . . I knew that he was a man after my own heart." [17] More than twenty years later, when the letters of William James were first published, Schiller gave this wonderful tribute to James:

> William James was a great man; the greatest, probably, who has yet taken birth in the Great Republic. He was also a great philosopher one of the half dozen who have made an epoch and given a new direction to the deepest, and dimmest, nisus of the human soul. But he was a great philosopher because he was a great man; a great man essentially, a philosopher consequentially.[18]

At one time, James wished that Schiller might serve for eternity as a professor in each reincarnation. (It seems necessary to add that James meant this as a compliment.)

There was, then, a warm personal relationship between these two men. Further, they had a profound mutual respect for each other's philosophical work. James referred to Schiller as "the only clear writer" on the pragmatic side.[19] James's response to *Riddles of the Sphinx*, 1891, was: "A book of great vigor and constructive originality, and quite in the lines which I incline to tread." [20] An essay by Schiller called forth the comment from James that it seemed "to be written with my own heart's blood—it is startling that two persons should be found to think so exactly alike." [21]

Many early discussions between James and Schiller concerned what name to give to this new philosophy and what the term pragmatism, this "blanket-word," was to cover. Should it refer only to the method? Might it be thought of as an equivalent term for radical empiricism? For humanism? James felt that the movement would have won its way to a better start "if our critics had been willing to wait until we got our message fairly out." [22] But the critics would not and did not stand on ceremony. Only a few months before his death, James wrote: "This is my doctrine and Schiller's, but its very hard to express it so as to get it understood." [23]

But in spite of the worries over the name and the troubles with the critics, James and Schiller went to battle with joy and confidence. James wrote to Schiller: ". . . How humanism will hum—drowning out the roar of the Russo-Japanese artillery across the Pacific." [24] James's son Henry wrote:

At the age of 63 he turned to the formulation of his empirical philosophy with the eagerness of a schoolboy let out to play. Misunderstanding disturbed him only momentarily, opposition stimulated him, he rejoiced openly in the controversies which he provoked, and engaged in polemics with the good humor and vigor that were the essence of his genius. His truth must prevail! the absolute should suffer its deathblow! Flourney, Bergson, Schiller, Papini, and others too were "on his side." He made merry at the expense of his critics . . . he always encouraged them to "lay on." . . . He expressed himself as freely as only a man can who has outgrown the reserves of his youth.[25]

Schiller enjoyed the polemics perhaps even more than James, and on more than one occasion James begged his English friend to go a little easy in his horseplay and polemical jeers. James was pleased when Schiller promised to temper his "gusto in controversy," and offered him this counsel: "Solemn as an owl and tender as a dove, should be your watchword from now on if you are to outlive these arrears of debt to the proprieties." [26]

The two men had their private jokes about their idealist opponents. James shared this one with Schiller in 1904. An American child asked his mother if it were true that God made the world in six days. The mother answered yes. And the child next asked: All of it? Again the mother answered yes. The child's next question: Then what is God's business now? The answer: Sitting for his portrait by Royce, Bradley, and Taylor.[27]

This, then, sketches in some of the atmosphere both beclouding and vitalizing the birth of pragmatism. It was a time when Schiller was recognized by Peirce and especially by James as a progenitor and a protector of pragmatism. Schiller was very much in evidence at the baptismal ceremony. He was unquestionably a member of the immediate family. On certain levels he antedated both James and Dewey as an explicator of this new philosophy. Much of the source material for this conclusion was published before the key philosophical works of Dewey appeared. One is tempted to say that Schiller was already a confirmed pragmatist when Dewey was yet an uncertain Hegelian.

The second lecture in William James's *Pragmatism*, 1907, is entitled "What Pragmatism Means." It is included in such anthologies as *Essays in Pragmatism,* edited by Alburey Castell, 1948; *The American Pragmatists,* edited by Konvitz and Kennedy, 1960; and *The Golden Age of American Philosophy,* edited by Charles Frankel, 1960. In that brief essay James placed the names of Dewey and Schiller either side by side or connected by *"and"* six times. This juxtaposition of names seems quite significant to a discussion of the beginnings of pragmatism. It is also perhaps of some significance that Dewey in an article bearing the similar title, "What Pragmatism Means by Practical"—which is part of his *Essays in Experimental Logic,* 1916—made no reference to Schiller.[28]

In addition to linking the names of James and Schiller as congenial cohorts in the founding of pragmatism, one could list many interests these two men shared. Both were involved with the solution of psychical problems. Both served, along with Henri Bergson, as presidents of the Society for Psychical Research. Both were deeply concerned with immortality. They had a common interest in such subjects as truth, metaphysics, religion, and so on. However, that which seems most germane to philosophy and to philosophy of education today is the existentialist emphasis so present in their philosophical writings.

This existentialist dimension in pragmatic philosophy has been rather thoroughly buried. The burial may have begun in 1916 with the publication of Dewey's *Democracy and Education.* More recent covering strata are to be found in Merle Curti's *The Social Ideas of American Educators,* both 1935 and 1959 editions; John Childs's *American Pragmatism and Education,* 1956; and Morton White's *Social Thought in America,* 1949 and 1957 editions. Perhaps Charles Frankel's *The Case for Modern Man* may also be considered as part of the submerging effort. This book does not oppose the general thesis of any of the above-mentioned works; the author is in fact in considerable sympathy with the tenets of each one of them. The point is that the existentialist, the personalist, and the individualist emphasis in early pragmatism got buried beneath a persistent and comprehensive social consideration. It is only in recent years that we have unearthed signs of the vital existentialist temper of early pragmatism.

This individualist character was obscured not only by writings but by such organizations as the Socialist party, the Liberal party, the Progressive Education Association, the Social Frontier thinkers, and the CIO in so far as it had a social philosophy. Each of the post-Wilsonian Democratic regimes in Washington was in its way social-minded, whatever may have been the personality of the man in the White House. The Republican opposition, while it may have been less social-minded whether in power or out, was even less cordial to what we may term the existentialist dimension in philosophy.

It may seem a paradox, but while the "social thinkers" were monopolizing the writing of historical accounts of philosophy, the "analytic thinkers" were beginning to take over the teaching of philosophy in the United States. Under the dual impasse of this condition, it could not be expected that existentialism would make much of an impression, whether its inspiration came from an American like James or from a European like Jaspers.

The covering strata over the James and Schiller existentialist dimension in pragmatism were many and of varying thicknesses. But by the 1950's and 1960's, the effect of the prodding of such Europeans as Kierkegaard and Nietzsche first, and then later Buber, Sartre, and Camus—also others to be sure—began to give existentialism its impact on American thought. John Wild became something of the historian of this impact, while Kaufmann and others became the anthologists of the new philosophical concern. Tillich and Maritain, European expatriates living in the United States, gave support; and William Barrett became a representative voice. All of this served to open up a way for the re-entry on the philosophic stage of the original existentialist impulse in James and Schiller.

Writing history is an all too open invitation to insert into the past that from the present which one would like to find there. The classic expression of this temptation was: Burn all the books for their wisdom is already contained in the wisdom of the Koran. This particular example may not have been much used in recent years, but someone has contended that the whole concept of the teaching machine was present in Socrates, and others profess to find the totality of existentialism in Saint Thomas. In our eagerness to justify the present or the past, we may read into the past what we *want* to find there rather than what *was* there. This book pleads innocent to this fallacy in claiming a substantial core of existentialism in James and Schiller.

According to William Barrett, the basic quality in existentialist philosophy is its holding that the particular is more significant than the universal.[29] As Kierkegaard put it: my category is the one. James habitually took the side of the concrete particular as opposed to the abstract universal. The following is indicative of his partiality:

> But alongside of this passion for simplification there exists a sister passion. . . . This is the passion for distinguishing; it is the impulse to be acquainted with the parts rather than to comprehend the whole. Loyalty to clearness and integrity of perception, dislike of blurred outlines, of vague identifications, are its characteristics. It loves to recognize particulars in their full completeness, and the more of these it can carry, the happier it is. It prefers any amount of incoherence, abruptness, and frag-

mentariness to an abstract way of conceiving things that, while it simplifies them, dissolves away at the same time their concrete fulness. . . . A man's philosophic attitude is determined by the balance in him of these two cravings.[30]

James's principal passion was for distinguishing, for the particular.

The Varieties of Religious Experience, first published in 1902, gives us a good insight into James's love and concern for the particular. From the Preface:

In my belief that a large acquaintance with particulars often makes us wiser than the possession of abstract formulas, however deep, I have loaded the lectures with concrete examples, and I have chosen these among the extremer expressions of the religious temperament.[31]

James turned to the extreme particular. Near the end of the book, we find James still staying with his love of the individual.

The less we mix the private with the cosmic, the more we dwell in the universal and impersonal terms, the truer heirs of Science we become.

In spite of the appeal which this impersonality of the scientific attitude makes to a certain magnanimity of temper, I believe it to be shallow, and I can now state my reason in comparatively few words. That reason is that, so long as we deal with the cosmic and the general, we deal only with the symbols of reality, but *as soon as we deal with private and personal phenomena as such, we deal with realities in the completest sense of the term.*

The world of our experience consists at all times of two

parts, an objective and subjective part. . . . The objective part is the sum total of whatever at any given time we may be thinking of, the subjective part is the inner "state" in which the thinking comes to pass. What we think of may be enormous,—the cosmic times and spaces, for example,—whereas the inner state may be the most fugitive and paltry activity of mind. Yet the cosmic objects . . . are but ideal pictures of something whose existence we do not inwardly possess . . . while the inner state is our very experience itself. . . .[32]

This may be the language of a nineteenth-century American psychologist, but surely the message is one suggestive of twentieth-century existentialists.

In the conclusion to *The Varieties of Religious Experience* we come upon a passage that points forward in time to Sartre. Perhaps it may bring Tillich to mind quicker than Sartre, but in any case we are not dealing with the conventional religious faith of the nineteenth and twentieth centuries. James held that the mistakes of our ancestors in matters of religion do not give us a reason to cease being religious. He said: "By being religious we establish ourselves in possession of ultimate reality at the only points at which reality is given us to guard. Our responsible concern is with our private destiny, after all." [33] If there is something of Tillich and his ultimate concern in the above, perhaps in what follows we catch some glimpse of Sartre as he discusses St. Genet. "Individuality is founded in feeling; and the recesses of feelings, the darker, blinder strata of character, are the only places in the world in which we catch real fact in the making, and directly perceive how events happen, and how work is actually done." [34]

In *The Will to Believe*, 1886, we find what appears to be an unmistakable existentialist ingredient. But, said Alburey Castell, "The right to believe on insufficient evidence, to exercise the will to believe, was currently denied and castigated by some philosophers speaking in the name of science." [35] Like James's contemporaries, present-day existentialists resist the scientist. There is a parallel between James's will to believe and the existentialist leap. An entry in Camus' notebook reads: "You cannot acquire experience by making experiments. You cannot create experience. You must undergo it." [36] This is the individualistic bias found both in James and in contemporary existentialists. One also finds clearly present James's voluntaristic side: " . . . That the will has a right to have its demands honored is a main theme in James' version of pragmatism." [37] James respected the emotions as well as the will, for to him " . . . every philosophy should be touched with emotion to be rightly understood." [38]

The following quotation from John E. Smith, although long, is included to bring out some of the existentialist temper found in William James.

Reading James is strenuous and not at all as easy as it is supposed to be. The reason is, happily, a creative one. His writing is a continual appeal to the individual to consult his own experience as a means of understanding and testing the ideas placed before him. . . . James constantly wrote as though one had only to consult "experience" as one consults a timetable in order to find the answer. . . .

Pragmatism stands as America's first indigenous philosophy, and William James's version of pragmatism is the one with which the largest number of people both at home and abroad seem to be acquainted. His position, expressing both a point of view and a solution to many classical philosophical problems, is no mere reworking of old ideas, but a fresh distillation of experience acquired on the American scene. Trusting his own experience and armed with the characteristically American concern for the vitality, variety, and challenging adventure of the world, James developed a philosophy of pluralism, radical empiricism, and voluntary assent. If Peirce's view of things was distinguished by his passion for logic and the universality we associate with mathematics, James's outlook was marked by a subordination of logic and the claim that living experience cannot be contained in any form of universal reason. While Peirce waxed eloquent over the need for a community of knowers and believers, James defended the uniqueness and irreducibility of the individual self. The hallmark of James's pragmatism is its uncompromising belief in each person's right, and even duty, to take his own experience seriously and use it as a touchstone for thought and action.[39]

Smith finds the heart of James's philosophy in a "consistent voluntarism." "Human intentions, purposes, plans, and goals are the dominant powers in his universe." [40]

For all the subjective bias, for all the voluntaristic overtones, for all the personalistic qualities, James remained and remains in the mainstream of American pragmatism. No one, so far as I know, has ever tried to read James out of the party. The same ingredients in Schiller, whether in greater or lesser intensities, have led to what we may term exile. Schiller is tagged a subjectivist, a voluntarist, a personalist, with the intent that these labels will place him beyond the pale of respectable and acceptable pragmatism. It must be readily admitted that some of Schiller's political notions are quite sufficient to have him forever banished from any self-respecting democratic group in the West. As Reuben Abel wrote:

Schiller's social philosophy was nothing less than fantastic. It was based on a consuming interest in eugenics . . . and on the alleged inability of the democracies to practice eugenics. It is worthy of comment that the chief American pragmatists have been convinced political and economic democrats, whereas Schiller's beliefs were quite the reverse. . . . His social and political views impress a reader of his other books as a wild and irrational vagary that has no connection, either logical or psychological, with the humanist core of his work. A metaphysics which regards the person as the ultimate reality certainly conforms more closely to democracy than to any other political philosophy. . . . His program of social reform is certainly more consonant with the views of quite other philosophic movements. But such speculation is properly outside the domain of philosophy.[41]

So much for Schiller's social thought; the less said about it, the better. But as philosopher qua philosopher, Schiller gets into trouble where James, doing pretty much the same sort of thing, reaps only praise. According to Abel, "The core of Schiller's vision is the conviction that all acts and thoughts are irreducibly the products of individual human beings and are therefore inescapably colored by the needs, desires and purposes of men." [42] With such a core, we need not be surprised that a good deal of Schiller's thinking displays a partiality to a position we should today label existentialism. Schiller maintained, " . . . It must never be forgotten that the immediate experience is after all in a way more real . . . than the 'higher realities' which are said to 'explain' it." [43] Schiller approximated the existentialist belief that "existence precedes essence," when he wrote: "It is not that we are because we think, but are able to think because we are." [44]

We may credit the existentialists with raising what Schiller called "burning questions" in philosophy. These men whom we group under existentialism, sometimes reluctantly on our part and sometimes reluctantly on their part, have tried to come to grips with problems that trouble men in general and not just philosophers in particular. They are not content to be mere technicians in the academy, and they have succeeded to some extent in restoring philosophy to the market place, where it has rarely been since Socrates. Schiller's list of burning questions, which he would have philosophers answer, has a good deal of similarity to the kind of questions existentialists have been working at.

> What should we mean by God? How are the various "Gods" related? How proved? What is the problem of evil? And why is it so difficult? Is life worth living; is death worth dying? What about a future life? [45]

Some of these questions must strike one as rather too inclined toward religion to be typical of Sartrean existentialist thought. This may well be; the point is that Schiller would put to the philosophers questions which disturb the sleep of Mr. Everyman.[46]

Over and over in Schiller the reader comes upon the great maxim of Protagoras: man is the measure of all things. While some existentialists may despair that man can measure anything, surely this is also their starting point. Sartre writes: "Man is nothing else but that which he makes of himself. This is the first principle of existentialism." [47] Subjectivity is a common word in Sartre; it is also a common word in Schiller.

As we look back from the 1960's toward the beginnings of pragmatism, we find Peirce introducing the idea in 1878, possibly 1871. James reintroduced it in 1898. By 1905, Peirce had decided to withdraw from the ranks of the main proponents of pragmatism. As we look over the movement prior to 1910, three names stand out above all others in the United States as actively engaged in developing and promulgating a new philosophic vision. They are James, Dewey, and Schiller. Of these three, James and Schiller seem more spontaneously, more emotionally, involved than Dewey. In the excitement of battle, Schiller was surely more deeply committed than Dewey at this very early stage. It is only fair to add, Dewey's commitment was the more enduring.

Further, if we look into these first years of pragmatism as exemplified by the work of James and Schiller for dominant moods, vital trends, then one tendency common to both of these men and retaining a considerable viability in the 1960's is what we today would call existentialism. This aspect of pragmatism may have been severely downgraded and even hidden during the period from 1910 to 1950. But this early existentialist content was no mere peripheral concern of F. C. S. Schiller and William James; rather, it was a central and deliberate part of pragmatism as developed by these two men.

1. John Dewey, *Philosophy and Civilization* (New York: Minton, Balch & Co., 1931), p. 13.

2. Philip P. Wiener (ed.), *Values in a Universe of Change: Selected Writings of Charles S. Peirce* (Garden City: Doubleday Anchor, 1958), p. 124.

3. W. B. Gallie, *Peirce and Pragmatism* (Harmondsworth, England: Penguin Books, 1952), pp. 13–14.

4. Quoted, *ibid.*, p. 14.

5. William James, *Pragmatism* (New York: Longmans, Green, & Co., 1929), p. 47.

6. *Ibid.*, p. 47.

7. Wiener, *op. cit.*, p. 186.

8. F. C. S. Schiller, "William James and the Making of Pragmatism," in Daniel Sommer Robinson (ed.), *An Anthology of Recent Philosophy* (New York: Thomas Y. Crowell, 1929), pp. 451–52.

9. *Op. cit.,* p. 14.

10. Bertrand Russell, *Sceptical Essays* (New York: Barnes & Noble Unwin Books, 1961), p. 42.

11. Gail Kennedy, "Pragmatism, Pragmaticism, and the Will to Believe—A Reconsideration," *Journal of Philosophy,* July 3, 1958, p. 582.

12. Kai Nielsen, "Dewey's Conception of Philosophy," *Massachusetts Review,* Autumn, 1960, p. 110.

13. John Dewey, *Character and Events* (New York: Henry Holt & Co. 1929).

14. Bertrand Russell, *A History of Western Philosophy* (New York: Simon & Schuster, 1945), p. 816. Copyright © 1945 by Bertrand Russell.

15. Ralph Barton Perry, *The Thought and Character of William James* (New York: Little, Brown & Co., 1935), II, 164.

16. *Ibid.,* II, 503.

17. F. C. S. Schiller, "William James and the Making of Pragmatism," in Robinson, *op. cit.,* p. 453.

18. F. C. S. Schiller, "William James," *Quarterly Review,* July, 1921, p. 42.

19. Perry, *The Thought and Character of William James,* II, 470.

20. *Ibid.,* II, 495.

21. Henry James (ed.), *The Letters of William James* (Boston: Atlantic Monthly Press, 1920), II, 271.

22. William James, *Pragmatism,* p. vii.

23. William James, *The Meaning of Truth* (New York: Longmans, Green & Co., 1909), p. 54.

24. Perry, *The Thought and Character of William James,* II, 505.

25. *The Letters of William James,* II, 246.

26. Perry, *The Thought and Character of William James,* II, 503.

27. Henry James (ed.), *The Letters of William James,* II, 216.

28. This sort of documentation may impress some readers as both unnecessary and naïve. But Schiller has been in such a state of eclipse that there is considerable obligation to document his former position in pragmatism as well as to hint at his neglect. For example, Philip P. Wiener in his *Evolution and the Founders of Pragmatism* (Cambridge:

Harvard University Press, 1949) makes no individual mention of Schiller. Corliss Lamont in his *Humanism as a Philosophy* (New York: Philosophical Library, 1949), carries this brief notation: "Still another version of Humanism was the subjective variety put forward at the beginning of this century by the late Oxford Don, the brilliant but erratic F. C. S. Schiller. Professor Schiller's humanism, borrowing from the more questionable elements in the pragmatism of William James, centered around a theory in which the personal, subjective factor was paramount and in which objective truth tended to melt away in the haze of moral and religious wish fulfillment. Schiller also made unacceptable compromises with supernaturalism" (p. 32). One may admire Lamont's frankness while wondering about his accuracy.

29. William Barrett, lecture at Mount Holyoke College, October 31, 1963.

30. Alburey Castell (ed.), *Essays in Pragmatism* (New York: Hafner Publishing Co., 1948), p. 5.

31. William James, *The Varieties of Religious Experience* (New York: New American Library, 1958), p. ix.

32. *Ibid.*, pp. 376–77.

33. *Ibid.*, pp. 378–79.

34. *Ibid.*, p. 379.

35. Alburey Castell, *op. cit.*, p. vii.

36. Albert Camus, *Notebooks—1935–1942* (New York: Alfred A. Knopf, 1963), p. 5.

37. Charles Frankel (ed.), *The Golden Age of American Philosophy*, p. 115.

38. James, *The Varieties of Religious Experience*, p. 337.

39. John E. Smith, *The Spirit of American Philosophy* (New York: Oxford University Press, 1963), pp. 39–41.

40. *Ibid.*, p. 41.

41. *The Pragmatic Humanism of F. C. S. Schiller*, pp. 145–47.

42. *Ibid.*, pp. 7–8.

43. F. C. S. Schiller, *Humanism* (London: Macmillan Co., 1903), p. 195.

44. F. C. S. Schiller, *Riddles of the Sphinx* (London: Macmillan Co., 1912), p. 47.

45. F. C. S. Schiller, *Our Human Truths*, p. 17.

46. See John Wild, *The Challenge of Existentialism* (Bloomington: Indiana University Press, 1955). "Academic philosophy has become a barren wasteland with little relevance to actual life and with little appeal, except to careerists and technicians" (p. 25). In the same volume Wild held that all that remained in philosophy is "logic and linguistic analysis" (p. 9), and that it was a "joy" to find existentialism (p. 7).

47. Jean Paul Sartre, *Existentialism* (New York: Philosophical Library, 1947), p. 18.

III. Must Pragmatists Disagree? Schiller and Dewey

Reuben Abel observed: "The hallmark of Schiller's life was that he constantly was swimming against strong philosophical currents." [1] The first current he swam against was the Hegelian idealism that dominated the English universities during his early academic years. Only a short time later, the opposing current was the rapidly rising school of symbolic logic. Schiller had the additional misfortune of swimming against strong currents within the very philosophy that he did so much to found. He had worked hard. "Actually, pragmatism was a great and difficult discovery," he wrote. "You can take this from me, because I had myself taken several steps on the way to it, before James blazed a trail that all could follow." [2] For all his heroic work, Schiller was often grouped with men of other philosophic dispositions. Schneider described Schiller's general position as that of "romantic personal idealism" and "subjective idealism." [3] Horace Kallen called him a "voluntarist." [4] Ralph Barton Perry thought of him as an "activist" and grouped him with Papini, Sorel, and Catholic modernists. [5]

Schneider even denied Schiller any intellectual comfort in his final years in California. "In his last years, which he spent at the University of Southern California, he had become too much of a humanist to please the personalist theists entrenched there." [6] For all of this, we note no sense of despair in Schiller. His wife, in the foreword to his last volume, spoke of the "vast contentment that settled over his later years." [7] A characteristic attitude of Schiller was that one can speak one's truth with a smile.

It was not long after the death of Schiller that a sort of Peirce revival occurred. Although Peirce had disengaged himself from pragmatism around 1905, and Dewey had taken over the priesthood of pragmatism after the death of James in 1910, a new philosophical climate, favorable to Peirce's analytic approach, developed in the 1940's and 50's. As Ludwig Wittgenstein, Rudolph Carnap, G. E. Moore, Bertrand Russell, A. J. Ayer, and their associates gained wide acceptance in American universities, a congenial environment was created for the reintroduction of Peirce. It was symptomatic of Peirce's analytic appeal that his first real impact had been made with an article entitled "How to Make Our Ideas Clear."

Of all the founders of pragmatism, Peirce lived, worked, and taught most alone. During his lifetime he had at best only a few isolated admirers. His teaching career at Johns Hopkins was brief and undistinguished. We are told he never had more than a dozen students in any of his classes there. He was refused an appointment at Harvard College. Most of his life was given to the U.S. Coast and Geodetic Survey and to writing countless articles that remained scattered until the 1930's, when the huge job of editing his *Collected Papers* began. Peirce, too, swam against the prevailing currents. Philip Wiener wrote:

Charles S. Peirce made it his life work to analyze, as thoroughly as any single mind could, the basic logic and structure of the sciences before committing himself to a philosophical world view or ethical conclusions about the human uses of science.

. . . William James is better known popularly and internationally than Charles Peirce because James wrote with more emotional appeal and literary skill in expressing his sensitivity to the common man's mental, moral, and religious problems; Peirce approached philosophy with the rarer and more technical instruments of exact logic, mathematical analysis, and the history of science and philosophy. Although James credited Peirce with the first formulation of pragmatism as a doctrine of meaning and method of inquiry, Peirce was more analytical and more precise than James. . . .[8]

Wiener held that in the field of symbolic logic, Peirce "stands with Boole, Frege, and Schroder as the forerunner of the calculus of propositions, classes, and relations."[9] The Introduction to his *Collected Papers* begins:

Charles Sanders Peirce plays a unique role in the history of American philosophy. During his own lifetime he published no book on philosophy, and except for a relatively short period he held no university chair from which to impress his influence upon students; yet he has come to be recognized as the founder of the one distinctive movement which this country has produced.

Pragmatism, as it developed, followed the pattern of William James' thought and that of John Dewey rather than the conceptions of Peirce; but it was Peirce, as James and Dewey magnanimously insisted, who defined the principle of the movement and gave it the first impetus. Never a leader of movements, Peirce was an originator of ideas. He clearly formulated in his writings many conceptions which are only today beginning to find recognition, and there are implications in his thought which have not yet been fully developed.[10]

This Introduction was written in 1931. We have good reason to believe that if it were to be written today, a more enthusiastic note would find its way into these opening comments.

The ninth entry in Volume I of his *Collected Papers* has the prophetic heading: The Analytic Method.

> The first problems to suggest themselves to the inquirer into nature are far too complex and difficult for an easy solution, even if any satisfactorily secure conclusion can ever be drawn concerning them. What ought to be done, therefore, and what in fact is done, is at first to substitute for those problems others much simpler, much more abstract, of which there is a good prospect of finding probable solutions. Then, the reasonable certain solutions of these last problems will throw a light more or less clear upon more concrete problems which are in certain respects more interesting. This method of procedure is that Analytic Method to which modern physics owes all its triumphs.[11]

Although he was perhaps somewhat less well disciplined in his personal life than the other founders, Peirce was above all the one who admired and strove for the disciplined mind. For him it was terrible "to see how a single unclear idea, a single formula without meaning, lurking in a young man's head, will sometimes act like an obstruction of inert matter in an artery, hindering the nutrition of the brain, and condemning its victim to pine away in the fullness of his intellectual vigor and in the midst of intellectual plenty." [12]

There was a considerable difference between James and

Peirce: James was psychologically oriented; Peirce was logically oriented. "Whereas Peirce sought the meaning of a proposition in its logical and experimentally testable consequences, James looked for more immediately felt sensations or personal reaction." [13]

The analytic dimension of Peirce, who died in 1914, had to wait the impact of the European logicians for a propitious reintroduction into American philosophy.

As Peirce's philosophic identity had to wait off stage for the arrival of Wittgenstein and company, so, in a sense, James's had to wait for the European existentialists to arrive on the American scene. As Peirce differed from James, who dominated pragmatism in its infancy, so James differed from Dewey, who dominated pragmatism during its ascendancy in American thought. William Barrett made a good deal out of these differences in his study of existential philosophy.

Of all the non-European philosophers, William James probably best deserves to be labeled an Existentialist. Indeed, at this late date, we may very well wonder whether it would not be more accurate to call James an Existentialist than a Pragmatist. What remains of American Pragmatism today is forced to think of him as the black sheep of the movement. Pragmatists nowadays acknowledge James's genius but are embarrassed by his extremes: by the unashamedly personal tone of his philosophizing, his willingness to give psychology the final voice over logic where the two seem in conflict, and his belief in the revelatory value of religious experience. There are pages in James that could have been written by Kierkegaard, and the Epilogue to *Varieties of Religious Experience* puts the case for the primacy of personal experience over abstraction as strongly as any of the Existentialists has ever done. James's vituperation of rationalism is so passionate that latter-day pragmatists see their own residual rationalism of scientific method thereby put in question. And it is not merely a matter of tone, but of principle, that places James among the Existentialists: he plumped for a world which contained contingency, discontinuity, and in which the centers of experience were irreducibly plural and personal, as against a "block" universe that could be enclosed in a single rational system.

Pragmatism meant something more and different for James than it did for Charles Sanders Peirce or John Dewey. The contrast between James and Dewey, particularly, shed light on the precise point at which Pragmatism, in the strict sense, ends and Existentialism begins. . . . The image of man as an earth-bound and time-bound creature permeates Dewey's writings as it does that of the Existentialists—up to a point. Beyond that point he moves in a direction that is the very opposite of Existentialism. What Dewey never calls into question is the thing he labels Intelligence, which in his last writings came to mean simply Scientific Method. Dewey places the human person securely within his biological and social context, but he never goes past this context into that deepest center of the human person where fear and trembling start. Any examination of inner experience—really inner experience—would have seemed to Dewey to take the philosopher too far away from nature in the direction of the theological. We have to remind ourselves here of the provincial and over-theologized atmosphere of America in which Dewey started his work, and against which he had to struggle so hard to establish the validity of a secular intelligence. . . . Dewey grew up in a period in which America was still wrestling with its frontier, and the mood of his writings is unshaken optimism at the expansion of our technical mastery over nature. Ultimately, the difference between Dewey and the Existentialists is the difference between America and Europe. The philosopher cannot seriously put to himself questions that his civilization has not lived.[14]

George Geiger, much closer to Dewey in his general philosophical orientation than Barrett, had a somewhat parallel criticism of Dewey.

There is almost nothing in his writings of anxiety, loneliness, anguish. The distressing experiences of humans all seem socially determined and socially controllable. . . . Lack of reference to personal torment and individual frustration makes for a certain thinness and unrealism in Dewey's writings. One is not expecting him to be an existentialist—although in a fellow pragmatist, William James, there is more than a little soul-searching—but one does miss, at least in these days, a necessary touch of forlornness.[15]

Dewey was so healthy-minded; we wonder what he would have done with a character like Genet—whom Sartre celebrated as an authentic human being.[16]

William Montague felt that the psychological faults in idealism were what inspired James's pragmatism, while the sociological and methodological faults in idealism were what aroused Dewey. This difference gave James a philosophy of "metaphysical pluralism stressing the free will and the independence of the individual." With Dewey, we have an instrumentalism that developed "into increasingly practicalistic treatises on education and social questions."[17] The following statement on the relationship between Dewey and James puts their differences perhaps even more strongly:

So far as I can see, with all Dewey's devotion to James as progenitor and liberator, with all of his sympathetic restatements of James's insights into forms more congenial to the trend of opinion and to the movement of his own philosophy, he never came to share James's feeling for the integrity of the unharmonizable and the irreconcilable, for the invincible spirit whose freedom is to stand helpless and alone before the omnipotent universe and choose annihilation rather than to yield. He never came to share James's feeling for the freedom which is experienced directly— . . . which intelligence cannot mediate; . . . Dewey never came to share James's sense of crisis in which simply not to yield is victory; or to agree that immediate vision can be knowing, that mystical experience is genuinely cognitive, that "supernatural" functions do occur in nature. Perhaps he never wanted to, nor could want to.

The paramount value in James's philosophic faith was that Freedom for which the word in other contexts is chance, contingency, plurality, novelty, with Reason derivative, operational, a working tool. The paramount value in Dewey's philosophic faith is Reason, whose right name is Intelligence, and whose work is to liberate by unifying, organizing, controlling, the kind of freedom to which James gives primacy.[18]

It seems obvious that pragmatism was not all of one piece as it originated in the United States at the turn of the century. Some of the initial differences have been buried for a while. It is the contention here that bringing these differences into public view in the 1960's would strengthen pragmatism rather than weaken it. Origins may well be more complex than endings, but the greater simplicity in endings may result from some undue pressures for conformity during the progress of a movement.

We have pointed up some of the differences between Peirce and James, and then some of the differences between James and Dewey. We now turn to a somewhat longer and more detailed examination of the differences between Dewey and Schiller. The sharpest contrast between these two men may be stated thus: Dewey was a social reformer; Schiller was not a social reformer. It is not that Schiller never played the role of the reformer. Probably no one in modern times ever tried harder than Schiller did to reform man's approach to the elusive idea of life after death. Probably no one worked harder at reforming logic than did Schiller. Two of his books are out-and-out reform tracts: *Eugenics and Politics,* 1926, and *Social Decay and Eugenical Reform,* 1932. In the latter book, Schiller spoke out: "Man must, therefore, remould himself, and transform himself into an altogether superior creature . . . if he is not to degenerate and perish." [19] Schiller had many ideas of reform that ranged from running eugenical baby shows to subsidizing members of parliament so they could propagate their superior minds and bodies. But the educational objectives of his reformist zeal were far removed in kind from the democratic purposes of John Dewey. Schiller's impulse was directed at an educated elite. He maintained: " . . . Our education must be *selective.* We must pick out the able and segregate them from the common herd. . . . One of the chief causes of educational waste and failure is the contamination of good, quick-witted minds by masses of dullness and stupidity." [20]

Dewey's aim in educational and other reform was to help society; Schiller's aim in reform was to help individuals, and only select individuals, at that. We need not worry here about Schiller as a reformer for he simply never had much success as a reformer. But John Dewey is another story altogether. Dewey succeeded as a reformer, and as a reformer he dominated pragmatism in the United States from (roughly) 1910, the death of James, to his own death in 1952.

If we consider, not how long Dewey dominated the pragmatic school, but rather how long he dominated American philosophy as a whole, then our estimate of his span of dominance must be confined to the period when pragmatism was dominant. Both Morton White and Charles Frankel name 1930 as the year when other forces began to usurp the reign of pragmatism in America. This would suggest that pragmatism held a paramount role in American philosophy for approximately twenty years, or even less, if we should date its ascendancy from the publication of *Democracy and Education* in 1916. While 1930 may be the year when the sovereign influence of pragmatism was first seriously threatened, it does seem that 1930 is too early a date to designate the successful challenger as either analysis, existentialism, or the neo-orthodoxy of Reinhold Niebuhr. At least we dare add three years to 1930, to bring us to a definite watershed: awareness of Adolph Hitler.

However one brackets the dates, Dewey clearly dominated both pragmatism and philosophy during the years when Schiller taught philosophy at the University of Southern California. And Dewey's supremacy imposed a societal emphasis in contrast to the personalist or existentialist emphasis that Schiller represented. According to Frankel, Dewey "went further than any of his predecessors in reinterpreting philosophy in social terms and spelling out the social and educational implications of the pragmatic method." [21] He "strenuously urged philosophers to leave the business of metaphysics for the industrial science of social engineering." [22]

Dewey probably pressed this emphasis of his philosophy rather too hard for many philosophers. Geiger, more in a mood of concern than of unfavorable criticism, took the position that if Dewey's philosophy seems dated, "it is most evident today in the field of politics," where " 'liberalism' seems almost a smear word." [23] Frankel found something just as alarming: " . . . What is unprecedented is that liberal voices should be speaking, as they now are, in such strange accents, in the accents of Burke and Kierkegaard and Dostoevsky and Heidegger. It is what gives substance to the feeling that something like an intellectual revolution is taking place." [24] It is more than thirty years since Dewey wrote *Liberalism and Social Action* and dedicated it to the memory of Jane Addams. Perhaps an intellectual revolution *has* taken place, especially in the field of politics.

Dewey and Schiller were in deep disagreement politically, as well as in the other ways that have been noted. But then, Schiller had known disagreement with fellow philosophers all his years. In 1934, he published a series of essays entitled *Must Philosophers Disagree?*, in which he declared that he welcomed disagreement. Disagreement, he said, is characteristic of philosophy. Philosophers are peculiar people "who excel ordinary folk quite as much in the oddities of their idiosyncrasies as in the profundities of their thought." [25] Schiller held that all real data arise from the personal context of "an individual soul" and that objectivity is always "factitious and fictitious." [26] To him, all minds are personal.

Hence Schiller was not upset that philosophers disagreed. He believed that " . . . any unity Philosophy can aim at will have to be of a very tolerant and elastic kind." [27] He had learned that in the most stubborn case, one can agree to differ. A practical recognition of relativity became, to him, "a matter of urbanity and manners, and only a bigot or a pedant can ignore it." [28]

In 1936, however, Schiller brought out an article entitled "Must Pragmatists Disagree?" Schiller could easily grant that philosophers of opposing beliefs must differ. But how far, he asked, "must such disagreement go among philosophers who have consented to wear the same labels?" [29] We are taken back to the differences between James and Dewey. Schiller felt that disagreements within the pragmatic ranks came from the differences

> between the pragmatists who drew their inspiration from William James and those who obtained their training in the Chicago school headed by Dewey. For some reason, not easily apparent, the latter often seem anxious to differentiate themselves from the former. But they never seem able to explain what precisely are their grounds for dissent. They content themselves with rehearsing a few rather obvious platitudes and ancient cliches, the application of which to the objects of their criticism is never specified. Strangely enough their attitude does not seem to be reciprocated by the former. These gulp down every extension or new application of pragmatic principles made by Professor Dewey with relish and without a qualm and appear to be merely puzzled why a line between the sheep and the goats should be drawn right through what appears to them to be essentially the same body of doctrines.[30]

Schiller called attention to the following eight points that seemingly divided the two sides:

1. The Chicago group (Dewey) stressed the social emphasis in knowledge and meaning. Schiller dismissed this difference with the note that the social nature of knowledge is "so obviously a commonplace" as to be taken for granted by every pragmatist.

2. The Dewey branch complained that the followers of James assumed that meaning is a private affair.

3. The Chicago men complained that Schiller was too much given to subjectivity. Schiller answered this objection by reminding them that all science is selection at its inception.

4. Schiller and his associates were accused of failing to take due notice of mathematics as a function of philosophy. Schiller replied that "to cherish animosity towards pure mathematics is about as impossible as to show disrespect towards the equator."

5. Schiller was accused of hostility toward formal logic. Schiller, with no way to escape this accusation, once again, as so often before, called logic a "pseudo-science and a word-game."

6. Professor Charles Morris of the Chicago group, according to Schiller, found "it difficult to reconcile my saying that the scientific method abstracts from personality with my pointing out that it does so for the purpose of arguing from one particular case to another; has it, then, never occurred to him that in order to obtain a general formula that can be transferred from case to case the particular circumstances of the first case (place, time, and personality) must be abstracted from?"

7. Morris would have given a higher place in pragmatism to Peirce than he then enjoyed. Schiller felt that Peirce had, over the years, grown increasingly mathematical and formalistic, and that this would be contrary to the Dewey emphasis since Dewey, too, was in protest against formalism in philosophy.

8. The final difference had to do with formal logic and probability. It was Schiller's conclusion that once mathematics becomes involved in an encounter with reality, mathematics itself becomes a discipline of probability.[31]

Apparently, these allegations of differences had been bothering Schiller for some time. Of course, each group had differences in addition to these. George Herbert Mead, who was very close to Dewey at Chicago and was once praised by Dewey as "the most original mind in philosophy in America of the last generation," differed from the others in his greater attention to anthropology. More recently, Paul Pfuetze discovered a "strange parallelism between the ego-alter dialectic of G. H. Mead's radically empirical philosophy and Martin Buber's religiously oriented reflections upon the I-Thou relation." He wrote, "It occurred to me that American pragmatism had been saying some of the same things that European *Existenz-philosophie* was emphasizing." [32] In all likelihood John Dewey never got around to reading with any great care either minor or major existentialist thinkers.

It is remarkable that so much has been rightfully credited to Dewey at Chicago. He was there but a single decade—1894–1904. Arthur Wirth observed:

In the 1890's Dewey saw that advances in scientific inquiry were confronting man with a crisis that involved the need to redefine the very nature of himself and his destiny. The sources of this were coming from all the sciences. Investigators on the Chicago campus were in the forefront of intellectual reconstruction and Dewey was in constant interaction with them.[33]

By the time Schiller's essay on pragmatic differences appeared, Dewey had long been at Columbia, but the name Chicago still stayed with him in connection with his role in formulating pragmatism. Perhaps at Columbia Dewey headed a more uniform school than he had at Chicago. At Chicago he was associated with peers; at Columbia we hear much more about him in relation to students.

Besides the marked differences between Dewey and Schiller, there were shades of differences between James and Schiller. But as Perry has said, it is not easy to formulate these differences between James and Schiller "because their philosophical doctrines are so inextricably interwoven with temperamental traits. The difficulty is aggravated by the fact James and Schiller . . . made every effort to consolidate their forces against the common enemy." [34]

Schiller, in outlining the eight differences that separated the James-inspired school of pragmatism from the Dewey-inspired school, did not seem to touch upon the critical factor separating the two schools. This factor, which made Schiller persona non grata, was reflected in the lifelong interest on the part of both James and Schiller in psychical research. The critical factor was their much more congenial attitude toward religion. There is a religious content in James's *The Will to Believe*, 1897, *Human Immortality*, 1898, and of course, *The Varieties of Religious Experience*, 1902. The titles of Schiller's books and articles scarcely suggest so much concern with religion, but the religious interest is clearly present in Schiller. We would not expect to find the following in the writings of John Dewey:

> I will candidly confess that to my thinking the question of immortality is one of the biggest, if not the biggest, question in philosophy and it is cowardice or worse in philoso-

phers not to face it. At the same time, it is not only a difficult but also a complicated question, and in many influential quarters a serious and dispassionate discussion of it is
by no means welcomed.[35]

Schiller saw the question as not only profoundly philosophical
but as downright practical. "Just as men arrange their lives
differently as they believe themselves to have one more year to
live or fifty, . . . so life must be ordered either on the assumption or the neglect of its indefinite prolongation and divine
care." [36]

But this topic does not figure greatly in man's studies.
Schiller speculated:

A visitor from Mars, dispassionately inquiring into human
conduct and motive, might find it hard to detect more
foreknowledge of death in men than in animals. From
palace to the hovel, from the laboratory to the oratory, he
would find men everywhere pursuing the ends of the
earth . . . while of the "other-worldliness," so often
preached and preached against in the literature, he would
hardly find a trace. . . . He would have to seek it, not in
the churches or the universities . . . but in the asylums
in which are secluded the unhappy victims of religious
mania or melancholy.[37]

Schiller wanted to go about the land and raise foundation
funds for the study of immortality. He asked why it should be
easier to raise funds for a hospital for leprous cats than for a
laboratory in which to test the prima facie evidence for human
immortality.

Dewey in a letter to James dated 1907 indicated his naturalistic orientation in matters of faith.

My own views are much more naturalistic, and a reaction against not merely intellectualistic and monistic idealism but against all idealism, except, of course, in the sense
of ethical ideals. Now, I seem to myself to be nearer you
than I am to Schiller at this point, yet I am not sure. On
the other hand, Schiller in his later writings seems to
emphasize that the good consequence which is the test of
an idea, is good not so much in its own right as in meeting
the claims of the idea, whatever the idea is. And here I
seem nearer to him than to you.[38]

This passage shows just how much searching went on among
the early pragmatists to find areas of agreement and areas of
differences. It expresses a spirit that seems not to have been
uppermost in the minds of American pragmatists by the time
Schiller wrote his essay "Must Pragmatists Disagree?"

A Common Faith comes as close as anything in Dewey's
writings to giving us Dewey's religious credo. In this small
book we find Dewey pleading for the religious but not for any
given religion: he wanted to see "the emancipation of the
religious from religion." [39] Here, Dewey gave us his definition
of God. He wrote: "It is this *active* relation between the ideal
and actual to which I would give the name 'God.' I would not
insist that the name *must* be given." [40] Corliss Lamont and
Sidney Hook were open in their hostility to orthodox beliefs.
Hook regarded naturalism as a philosophy "sufficient to gratify
all the legitimate needs of the understanding," and considered
that where it was found to fall short was in its failure to
provide "the consolation which the tender-minded must
have." [41]

The revival of religion today is not due to the discovery
of new arguments or evidence for super-naturalism or a

profounder analysis of the logic of religious belief. This is apparent in the fact that among intellectuals it is not rational theology but mystical theology, not the principle of objectivity but of subjectivity, not the clear, if defective arguments of Aquinas but the record of the tormented inner experience of Augustine, Pascal, Kierkegaard which are found most appealing.[42]

It is remarkable how this brief passage from Hook brings once more into focus the differences that were noted in our discussion of the differences between James and Dewey, and how also the existentialists reappear.

Schiller had a definition of religion rather closely paralleling the definition Dewey gave us of the term God. Schiller saw religion "as the soul's aspiration towards an ideal wherewith to rectify and transfigure the actual." [43] He was a good deal more permissive than was Dewey in assignment of uses to the word God.

. . . The title of "God" can be bestowed upon whatever any one is willing to worship as divine. It is just this attitude of adoration which practically follows from the appellation "God." Which is why the human race has worshiped so many, and such queer, gods, and why Professor Alexander can attribute "deity" to any not yet intelligible novelty that "emerges" from the matrix of Space-Time.[44]

Schiller showed plainly his pragmatic colors when he wrote, " 'God' is a postulate, or rather a number of postulates, to be tested, like all postulates, by its working." [45] Of course, some pragmatists are not prepared to test at this level of operation.

We are in our day rather too inclined to identify psychical

research with the religious or with the superstitious impulse. For Schiller, this research was motivated by more than these impulses. It was connected with his pluralism, with his science, and even, one may suppose, with his sense of humor.

> Hence a philosophy which reckons seriously with the metaphysical possibility of pluralism and with the psychological ultimacy of personal experience, will think twice before it assumes without further ado that the present universe of physics is all the being there is, and that the human soul is inextricably entangled in it and cannot conceivably arise above it.[46]

Schiller found that living a mere terrestrial life on a tiny planet attached to a star, itself lost in the immensities of space, "Can never be made to seem sufficiently significant and satisfactory to be acceptable as the whole meaning of life." [47] Philosophically, Schiller held, "there is nothing to hinder us from recognizing an indefinite plurality of worlds, with a series of transitions into worlds of higher reality and greater value." [48] All of this sounds quite un-Dewey-like.

But Schiller did not find any serious conflict between his psychical interests and his pragmatic orientation. He would have put the question of man's immortality to the scientific test. He fully intended to have the scientific method applied to the full range of psychical problems. Of course, there would be some difficulties. For one, in the field of psychical research, "we can experiment not at all, or hardly at all." [49] He advised, however, that we should not despair, for we are just beginning; we are at what he called the groping stage. Even in his lifetime, he saw progress. He could remember when to take part in such research was to "incur an imputation of insanity." [50]

But he saw the problems in this area as not all on the earthly side of the great divide. If one is dealing with a beyond, one has increased one's own problems by adding to them those of the other world or worlds.

> Psychical Research is far from popular on earth. There are pretty good reasons why it should be even more unpopular in the beyond. No one can seriously and honestly contend that it is a good thing that we should know nothing about what death means to us. . . . But it is easy to conceive that once the ordeal of death is passed, it may seem in a high degree repugnant, unnecessary, and degrading to allow one's thoughts to dwell on the dreadful past and to attempt to resume relations with a world like ours.
> In trying to establish communications with other worlds we are probably dealing with forces which are not seriously interested in us, or nothing like as much as we are in them; at present these forces are beyond our control.[51]

Schiller was not one to give up easily. He went about searching for evidence of an afterlife as deliberately as we go about our huge chemical laboratories looking for new ways to kill houseflies and to find longer-lasting deodorants. "If we desire knowledge, then, we must work for it—in psychical research as elsewhere."[52] One may wonder whether psychical research at the present time enjoys leadership of the high caliber that it had under Bergson, James, and Schiller.

Schiller wanted to be just as scientific in religion as in psychical research. He wrote: "Religious truths also will begin their careers as postulates, and will need, and will receive, verification by experience. And they will attest their truth by the manner of working . . . rather than by their success in evolving verbally invulnerable formulas. . . . "[53] This sort of statement could have made Schiller unpopular among the orthodox believers in supernatural religion as well as among his pragmatic associates in philosophy departments.

Stephen White, in his doctoral dissertation on Dewey and Schiller, made Schiller's religious inclinations the aspect of thought that most sharply differentiated these two men. He said, "Schiller's belief in a personal God, personal immortality, and religious experience as unique, indicates that he makes a decided place for the supernatural."[54] Dewey, he wrote, was "wholly at odds with Schiller as to individual immortality." White called Schiller's brand of humanism "a glorified or universalized fideism."[55] Fideist has been used to describe James's position as well as that of Schiller. Dewey, of course, was far removed from any fideism. Dewey did not permit anything that opposed his empirical naturalism "to step in and become a part of his philosophy."[56] Schiller, on the contrary, looked to religion not only to support his fideism—if that is the best term for his belief—but to bolster up his commitment to pragmatism. He said, "Religious phenomena will supply no small part of the evidence to which the humanists' theory makes appeal."[57] We may be certain that no one from the Chicago school, whether an original member or a descendant from that group, would accept this statement.

It may be useful here to turn once more to William James in order to show that Schiller was not a great oddity in the pragmatic ranks on this matter of religion. James, too, felt that the human world as we know it may be just one of many. He, too, was concerned with the same or related problems in the field of psychical research. James wrote: "I have myself collected hundreds of cases of hallucinations in healthy persons.

The result is to make me feel that we all have potentially a 'subliminal' self, which may make at any time an irruption into our ordinary lives." [58] Sooner or later he believed religion would drive irreligion to the wall because religion lends support to the vigorous life. "The Capacity of the strenuous mood lies so deep that even if there were no metaphysical or traditional grounds for believing in a God, men would postulate one simply as a pretext for living hard, and getting out of the game of existence its keenest possibilities of zest." [59] In his belief that religious fermentation is always a symptom of the intellectual vigor of a society, he held that it is only when religions forget "they are hypotheses and put on rationalistic and authoritarian pretensions, that our faiths do harm." [60] Since "our science is a drop, our ignorance a sea," it is our human duty not to place a limit upon our possibilities. He wrote, "A man's religious faith means for me essentially his faith in the existence of an unseen order of some kind in which the riddles of the natural order may be found explained." [61]

Dewey had little of this sort of writing in him. These were not the drums he heard. Religion, as we usually understand that aspect of human life, stood as an obstacle to Dewey's vision of democracy. He maintained, "I cannot understand how any realization of the democratic ideal as a vital and spiritual ideal in human affairs is possible without surrender of the conception of the basic division to which supernatural Christianity is committed." [62] Dewey's continuing war against dualism wherever he found it did not allow him to indulge in any such two worlds as the natural and supernatural, let alone the plurality of worlds that made its way into the thinking of James and Schiller.

White would explain the wide divergencies between these pragmatists on the basis of each one's view of experience. He wrote, "Undoubtedly the determining factor for Schiller is

personality." [63] According to White, Schiller followed the subjective and Dewey the objective strain in James's psychology.
Abel said the same thing. To White, the psychology of Schiller
was individualistic rather than social. "Everything is relative to
the individual." [64] Schiller himself put it in these words: "In all
real knowing the personal equation always plays a part. You
may dislike this fact, . . . but you cannot deny it, unless you
are bent on giving a stupendous example of personal prejudice
yourself. And then you signally prove the very point you were
trying to contest." [65] According to White, the terms we find in
Schiller are "psychological, mentalistic, subjectivistic," while
those in Dewey are "objectivistic, behavioristic, and logical." [66]
Schiller said "Actual experience is always grouped around a
personal self." [67] Dewey expressed his social viewpoint thus:

> We often fancy that institutions, social customs, collective
> habits have been formed by the consolidation of individ-
> ual habits. In the main this supposition is false to fact. To
> a considerable extent customs, or widespread uniformities
> of habit, exist because individuals face the same situation
> and react in like fashion. But to a larger extent customs
> persist because individuals form their personal habits
> under conditions set by prior customs. An individual
> usually acquires the morality as he inherits the speech of
> his social group. The activities of the group are already
> there. . . . Each person is born an infant, and every in-
> fant is subject from the first breath he draws and the first
> cry he utters to the attentions and demands of
> others. . . . Few persons have either the energy or the
> wealth to build private roads to travel upon. They find it
> convenient, "natural," to use the roads that are already
> there; while unless their private roads connect at some
> point with the high-way they cannot build them even if
> they would.[68]

We could hope for no more obvious a differentiation between Dewey and Schiller at this social-versus-individual level.

White's effort at psychological differentiation between these pragmatists seems quite unsatisfactory. However, of all oversimplifications, the psychological ones may be the most tempting and at the same time the most misleading. White has suggested that Dewey was an "extrovert," while Schiller was an "introvert." Kallen, who knew Dewey well, found him to be "always shy, deliberate, hesitant in speech and not often graceful in expression." [69] These would scarcely be the manners of an extrovert. Edwin Slosson, in a published profile of Schiller, reported: "Schiller is as interesting to converse with as to read, that is more than you can say of many authors. He talks best while in motion, a real peripatetic philosopher." [70] Further, Slosson said that so far as he knew, Schiller was the "first philosopher to find room for jokes in his formal philosophy." [71] Dr. E. G. C. Poole, who knew Schiller in Switzerland, said that Schiller was much given to puns, even bad ones, and that he frequently came forth "with comments of real Voltairean pungency." [72] These would hardly be the communications of an introvert.

Schiller must have anticipated a possible carelessness on the part of a biographer. Of himself he observed, "I speak with some feeling, as one who does not greatly relish the prospect of nourishing some parasitic historian after his demise." [73] White should *not* be considered a parasitic historian, but he may have been careless when he used "introvert" and "extrovert" personality structures to explain the differences between Dewey and Schiller. Even so, Schiller might have welcomed a psychological interpretation, for he also wrote, "And the reason so many philosophies remain mysteries is precisely because we cannot reconstruct the psychology of their authors." [74]

White offered a more plausible character distinction with

his suggestion that the Oxford atmosphere made Schiller a different sort of man from what he would have been had he spent most of his life at an American university. Near the end of his life, Schiller found a home, a garden, and a wife in California, but he remained thoroughly European. He was even called "much more European than English." [75] By contrast, Dewey was about as American as a man can be. He did not even stay a Hegelian for long. The lack of graduate students at Schiller's Oxford and their great concentration at Dewey's Chicago and Columbia might have induced some disparate habits, but probably would have produced no very profound effects upon the two men's philosophies.

The purpose here is not so much to account for the differences between these two philosophers as it is to bring their differences into focus. Any scheme of matching opposites has its dangers, as we have just seen in White's introvert and extrovert construct. If we used James's categories of tender-minded and tough-minded, we should have to place Dewey on the tough-minded side and put Schiller somewhere on the tender-minded side. If we used a continuum from social to individual, we should place each man in a polar position, one at one end and the other at the other end. On a line from fascist to democratic, there would be a good deal of space between Schiller and Dewey. This by no means exhausts the scales on which each would show a wide divergence from the other in generalized philosophical attitudes and dispositions.

When we turn to more specific aspects of the work of these two thinkers, however, we find that they have a great deal in common—much more than one might be led to believe from the last several pages.

Schiller was no less an opponent of absolutes than Dewey. He contended, "The eternal truths, unable to sustain the pace, have long ceased to reside with us." [76] Nothing, he held, "can be said to be absolutely exempt from modification and amendment by experience of its working." [77] His position on the quest for certainty was much the same as Dewey's. It was this: "Actual thinking, no doubt, conducts only to practical, not to absolute, certainty (whatever that may mean); but it is enough to live by, and is what we all do live by. . . ." [78]

Schiller found the wonderful thing about truth to be precisely that it is not absolute, for then we could not improve upon it. "A truth may grow more probable and certain throughout the ages, without ever becoming absolute." [79] He advised that men be satisfied with this approach to truth and not go about in a mad search for the chimera of absolute truth. "Absolute truth is nothing but a snare which catches the dramatic. It is a meaningless illusion which no human knowledge guarantees." [80] The examples of Schiller's stand against absolute truth may be found throughout his writings. They compare favorably in intensity of opposition and vigor of expression with anything to be found in Dewey.

Similarly, both philosophers were opposed to pure knowing or pure knowledge. "For what is given man in knowing is reality-relation-to-him, and reality-per-se is an inference and a construction in which the nature and the activity of the human mind are plainly implicated." [81] In our times we have heard much about value-free research, about pure science; there are those observers who would be so pure that they would eliminate themselves. But Schiller scoffed, "Even if Theory is made so 'pure' as to become inapplicable altogether and thereby meaningless, it will at least have the practical effect of alienating from reality the mind that entertains itself by playing with it." [82]

The pure scientist is always up against a plurality of theoretical problems; but as soon as he makes up his mind to study one and not another, the purity vanishes—if it ever existed. Schiller pointed out: "Our knowing is always operational. It is never merely passive and random 'observation.' . . . It is always more or less experimental. It is false, therefore, that our knowing makes no difference to the objects it knows." [83] With Dewey, Schiller disliked any dualism separating theory from practice. "The whole antithesis between Theory and Practice is thoroughly false and misleading." [84]

For years Dewey has been known as the great friend of the scientific method. Until some recent shifts brought on by the philosophy of analysis, Dewey was saluted as the philosopher of science. For example, he wrote:

> Here, then, lies the reconstructive work to be done by philosophy. It must undertake to do for the development of inquiry into human affairs and hence into morals what the philosophers of the last few centuries did for the promotion of scientific inquiry in physical and physiological conditions and aspects of human life.[85]

Probably not many are aware of how closely Schiller approximated this view about the place of science in human affairs. Surely, little that Dewey wrote went far beyond the following statement on scientific method by Schiller in 1930:

> The application of Scientific Method is universal. Despite the attempts of certain scientists to represent it as something exclusive and mysterious, there is nothing too lowly, repulsive, obscure, contentious, or deceptive to come within its scope. Neither is there anything too "sacred," which generally means a fear that things so denominated cannot bear investigation. The Scientific Method is

the only genuine method of knowing, and will tackle anything knowable. It despises no problem and prejudges no question. It is willing to begin operations on any material it can get, however insecure, dubious, or dull, and pry into lingering pseudo-sciences like astrology, heraldry, and Formal Logic as zealously as into the most flourishing and progressive sciences. For it has enough confidence in itself to shrink from nothing, and to be capable of learning from anything.[86]

And this is about as Deweyan as another author's statement can be: "It is not too much to say that on one side Pragmatism means the discovery by Philosophy of the methods of Science." [87]

It was no accident that Schiller was asked to contribute to both volumes of *Studies in the History and Methods of Science.* In his essay in the earlier volume, 1917, Schiller pleaded for a science "that can handle human life and meet human needs." [88]

In any long-term evaluation of Schiller, one should probably say that his greatest contribution came in the field of logic. Here, too, he and Dewey traveled similar roads. Schiller's effort to formulate a logic of discovery had much in common with Dewey's effort to develop a logic of inquiry. While Dewey did not once mention Schiller in his *Logic,* it is possible to think that Schiller's unending attack on formal logic may have encouraged Dewey to write his large volume on logic. Schiller called formal logic "nonsense fortified by technicality" and a "dull rehearsal of barren and worthless technicalities" [89] and a discipline dedicated to the "avoidance of risk." [90] But in actuality, he believed, our world is contingent, our axioms are postulates, our truth is composed of probabilities, and novelties are forever entering this universe with the lid off. He said:

We must steel ourselves to face a future that is really
contingent, and really capable of generating novelties. We
are armed only with probable anticipations; but it rests
with us to cultivate a plasticity of mind that will keep pace
with the changes of the real and readily adjust itself to
new conditions.[91]

The world never has been presented to man on a platter of
formal logic. Therefore, he held: "Since we do not know what
the world is, we have to find out. This we do *by trying.*" [92]
"Trying" meant to Schiller what it meant to Dewey—that we
test our truths, our theories, by experiment, by action, by
consequences. "The official definition of pragmatism, that the
truth of any assertion depends on its consequences, looks innocent enough. . . . Its real meaning is that all knowledge is
empirical, and that no sort of formal logic is desirous or capable
of dealing with real truth at all." [93] The question of truth is
"primarily a practical one." [94] Schiller would have us take to
the offense. "But from the experimenting itself there is no
escape; it goes on, and if we refuse to experiment, *we are
experimented with.*" [95] We come to our truths by experimentation, not by formal logic. As Schiller saw it, formal logic proved
itself "quite impotent to diminish the amount of bad reasoning
in the world. Logic has been merely a source of pride in
pedants and an instrument of educational torture." [96] Dewey's
writings on this same problem have much in common with the
passages just quoted from Schiller. Dewey wrote:

Scientific principles and laws do not lie on the surface of
nature. They are hidden, and must be wrested from nature
by an active and elaborate technique of inquiry. Neither
logical reasoning nor the passive accumulation of any
number of observations—which the ancients called experi-

ence—suffices to lay hold of them. Active experimentation must force the apparent facts of nature into forms different to those in which they familiarly present themselves; and thus make them tell the truth about themselves, as torture may compel an unwilling witness to reveal what he has been concealing. Pure reasoning as a means of arriving at truth is like the spider who spins a web out of himself. The web is orderly and elaborate, but it is only a trap. . . .

A logic of discovery . . . looks to the future. Received truth it regards critically as something to be tested by new experiences rather than as something to be dogmatically taught and obediently received. Its chief interest in even the most carefully tested ready-made knowledge is the use which may be made of it in further inquiries and discoveries. Old truth has its chief value in assisting the detection of new truth.[97]

This matching operation could be carried to great length. But the purpose here is not to compile an exhaustive list of parallels in the thought of John Dewey and F. C. S. Schiller. Rather the intent is to show that once we go beyond certain generalized differences of a high order of abstraction, we encounter a striking similarity of approach and emphasis. One may find psychical research quite offensive in a pragmatist; one may feel that the personalism is excessive. But when we read Schiller on absolutes, on science, on logic, then perhaps even the most Deweyan of us may give a reassured and reassuring cheer for the work of the Englishman.

Dewey called first for a reconstruction in philosophy and then for a reconstruction of philosophy. Schiller hoped for changes. To Schiller, philosophy had gone to rest in "the super-celestial regions where Pure Thought subsists on the supersensible aether and deathless Forms are gorged with nectar and ambrosia." [98] He feared that his subject might "sink out of sight in the mire of academic pedantry." [99] He was worried that philosophy was "already perilously near the danger-point at which a subject grows unteachable." He asked his university colleagues: ought we not be aware of "pushing it over the brink?" [100]

It was Schiller's conclusion, in his day, that pragmatism could save philosophy from going over the brink. Pragmatism, he said, had "restored to philosophy its contact with everyday life and with the working sciences. Philosophy is no longer doomed to be an idle game of contemplation, juggling with verbal counters, whose only use is to minister to the superiority-complex of its adepts." [101] He hoped that pragmatism had emancipated philosophy from "the dead hand of pedantry."

Schiller set up a program that he felt would rescue philosophy. First, philosophy had to rid itself of the notion that being useless was its merit, for " . . . to proclaim a study useless is to damn it in the eyes of the people." Second, philosophy should present its material with "greater lucidity" and in "a simple style." Third, it could get along with less history of philosophy. And, finally, it was time to take more interest in the sciences and the problems with which they dealt. [102] Dewey could have stamped his approval on each of these suggestions.

This chapter opened with the observation that Schiller seemed destined during his lifetime to swim against strong philosophical currents. We might find the currents today somewhat more congenial. But how can we get him into some stream of American philosophy—if not the mainstream, at least that eddy which we might call the reading list for undergraduates? With our great increase in college enrollments, there must be many students who just are not equipped to read Ayer, Moore, Wittgenstein, and other analytics. Among them, there must be a number who are not in the mood to take on Sartre or Kierkegaard. Dewey might prove a little dull to them at this stage—dull as a stylist, that is.

Today there may be quite a large audience of undergraduates for Schiller. He reads easily. He is witty. His remarks continue to have relevance. One barrier to his return is posed in the question, Must pragmatists disagree? If we can accept the thesis of this book that pragmatism is made up of three concerns—the analytic as with Peirce, the reformist as with Dewey, and the existentialist as with James and Schiller—then perhaps some of the hostility and some of the indifference to Schiller can be dissipated. Then perhaps we can have the Schillerian wit present on our campuses to persuade our undergraduates that philosophy need not be dull or overburdened with technicalities. We probably do not have to fear, at this particular time, that philosophy is about to go over the brink or disappear in a pedantic mire. But there does seem to be some danger that philosophy may become either the private province of a highly gifted minority who are concerned only with its technical aspects or the public platform of a highly verbal minority who quote passages from Heidegger or Sartre at the drop of a concept without any regard for the relevance.

1. *The Pragmatic Humanism of F. C. S. Schiller*, p. 4.

2. F. C. S. Schiller, *Must Philosophers Disagree?* (London: Macmillan Co., 1934), p. 73. All quotations from this work are used by permission of the publisher.

3. Herbert W. Schneider, *A History of American Philosophy* (New York: Columbia University Press, 1946), p. 528.

4. Horace M. Kallen, "Pragmatism," *The Encyclopedia of the Social Sciences* (New York: Macmillan Co., 1934), XII, 310.

5. Ralph Barton Perry, *The Thought and Character of William James* (Boston: Little, Brown & Co., 1935), II, 581.

6. Schneider, *op. cit.*, p. 528.

7. Louise S. Schiller, Foreword to F. C. S. Schiller, *Our Human Truths*, p. vii.

8. Philip P. Wiener (ed.), *Values in a Universe of Chance*, p. xiii.

9. *Ibid.*, p. xiv.

10. Charles Hartshorne and Paul Weiss (eds.), *Collected Papers of Charles Sanders Peirce* (Cambridge: Harvard University Press, 1960), p. 118.

11. *Ibid.*, p. 27.

12. Wiener, *op. cit.*, p. 118.

13. *Ibid.*, p. 181.

14. William Barrett. From IRRATIONAL MAN, copyright © 1958 by William Barrett. Reprinted by permission of Doubleday & Company, Inc., and Heinemann Educational Books Ltd., London.

15. George R. Geiger, *John Dewey in Perspective* (New York: Oxford University Press, 1958), p. 160.

16. Jean Paul Sartre, *Saint Genet—Actor—Martyr* (New York: George Braziller, 1963). In this book Sartre wrote: "Genet's dignity is the demand for evil," p. 55.

17. William Montague, "The Story of American Realism," in Dagobert D. Runes (ed.), *Twentieth Century Philosophy* (New York: Philosophical Library, 1943), p. 421.

18. Horace M. Kallen, "John Dewey and the Spirit of Pragmatism," in Sidney Hook (ed.), *John Dewey: Philosopher of Science and Freedom* (New York: Dial Press, 1950), pp. 37–38.

19. F. C. S. Schiller, *Social Decay and Eugenical Reform* (London: Constable & Co., 1932), p. vi.

20. *Ibid.*, p. 91.

21. Charles Frankel (ed.), *The Golden Age of American Philosophy*, p. 382.

22. Morton White, *Social Thought in America*, p. 146.

23. Geiger, *op. cit.*, p. 163.

24. Charles Frankel, *The Case for Modern Man* (Boston: Beacon Press, 1959), p. 43.

25. *Must Philosophers Disagree?*, p. 12.

26. *Ibid.*, p. 6.

27. *Ibid.*, p. 11.

28. *Ibid.*, p. 163.

29. Schiller, *Our Human Truths*, p. 57.

30. *Ibid.*, p. 57.

31. *Ibid.*, pp. 58–64.

32. Paul Pfuetze, *Self, Society, and Existence* (New York: Harper & Row, Publishers, 1961), p. 1.

33. Arthur G. Wirth, "John Dewey's Design for American Education: An Analysis of His Work at the University of Chicago, 1894–1904," Washington University, 1964 (mimeographed), p. 2.

34. Perry, *The Thought and Character of William James*, II, 494.

35. Schiller, *Our Human Truths*, p. 141.

36. F. C. S. Schiller, *Humanism* (London: Macmillan Co., 1903), p. 230.

37. *Ibid.*, pp. 233–34.

38. Schneider, *op. cit.*, p. 553.

39. John Dewey, *A Common Faith* (New Haven: Yale University Press, 1960), p. 27.

40. *Ibid.*, p. 51.

41. Sidney Hook, *The Quest for Being* (New York: St. Martins Press, 1961), p. 98.

42. *Ibid.*, p. 96.

43. Schiller, *Must Philosophers Disagree?*, p. 312.

44. Schiller, *Problems of Belief* (London: Hodder & Stoughton, 1924), p. 145.

45. Schiller, *Must Philosophers Disagree?*, p. 297.

46. *Ibid.*, p. 286.

47. *Ibid.*, p. 285.

48. *Ibid.*, p. 286.

49. *Ibid.*, p. 324.

50. *Ibid.*, p. 321.

51. *Ibid.*, pp. 335–36.

52. F. C. S. Schiller, "Truth and Psychical Research," *Nineteenth Century*, July, 1927, p. 64.

53. Schiller, *Must Philosophers Disagree?*, p. 313.

54. Stephen Solomon White, "A Comparison of the Philosophies of F. C. S. Schiller and John Dewey" (Chicago: University of Chicago Libraries, 1940), p. 58.

55. *Ibid.*, p. 67.

56. *Ibid.*, pp. 23–24.

57. Schiller, *Must Philosophers Disagree?*, p. 313.

58. William James, *The Will to Believe* (New York: Longmans, Green & Co., 1931), p. 322.

59. *Ibid.*, p. 213.

60. *Ibid.*, p. xii.

61. *Ibid.*, pp. 51–52.

62. Dewey, *A Common Faith*, p. 84.

63. White, *op. cit.*, p. 22.

64. *Ibid.*, p. 19.

65. Schiller, *Must Philosophers Disagree?*, p. 309.

66. White, *op. cit.*, p. 37.

67. Schiller, *Must Philosophers Disagree?*, p. 6.

68. John Dewey, *Human Nature and Conduct* (New York: Modern Library, 1930), pp. 58–59.

69. "John Dewey and the Spirit of Pragmatism," p. 28.

70. Edwin E. Slosson, "A British Pragmatist: The Philosophy and Personality of F. C. S. Schiller," *Independent*, February 12, 1917, p. 265.

71. *Ibid.*, p. 265.

72. Quoted in R. R. Marett, "Ferdinand Canning Scott Schiller," *Proceedings of the British Academy*, XXIII, 10.

73. Schiller, *Must Philosophers Disagree?*, p. 10.

74. *Ibid.*, p. 10.

75. Quoted in Marett, *op cit.*, p. 8.

76. F. C. S. Schiller, "Axioms as Postulates," in Henry Sturt (ed.), *Personal Idealism* (London: Macmillan Co., 1902), p. 104.

77. *Ibid.*, p. 57.

78. F. C. S. Schiller, *Logic for Use* (New York: Harcourt, Brace & Co., 1930), p. 33. All quotations from this work are used by permission of the original publishers, G. Bell & Sons Ltd., London, England.

79. *Ibid.*, p. 319.

80. Schiller, *Our Human Truths,* p. 296.

81. Schiller, *Must Philosophers Disagree?,* p. 288.

82. *Ibid.*, p. 181.

83. *Ibid.*, p. 288.

84. *Ibid.*, p. 181.

85. John Dewey, *Reconstruction in Philosophy* (New York: New American Library, 1950), p. 18.

86. Schiller, *Logic for Use,* p. 386.

87. Schiller, *Must Philosophers Disagree?,* p. 71.

88. F. C. S. Schiller, "Scientific Discovery and Logical Proof," in Charles Singer (ed.), *Studies in the History and Method of Science* (Oxford: Clarendon Press, 1917), I, 288.

89. Schiller, *Logic for Use,* p. 48.

90. *Ibid.*, p. 47.

91. Schiller, *Must Philosophers Disagree?,* p. 213.

92. Schiller, "Axioms and Postulates," p. 55.

93. Schiller, *Must Philosophers Disagree?,* pp. 306–7.

94. Schiller, *Logic for Use,* p. 95.

95. Schiller, "Axioms and Postulates," pp. 57–58.

96. Schiller, *Must Philosophers Disagree?,* p. 307.

97. Dewey, *Reconstruction in Philosophy,* pp. 48–49.

98. Schiller, *Must Philosophers Disagree?,* p. 47.

99. *Ibid.*, p. vi.

100. *Ibid.*, p. 49.

101. *Ibid.*, p. 71.

102. *Ibid.*, pp. 36–38.

IV. Pluralism and the Pluralistic Temperament

Philosophers no longer seek to find true being in the One, which is both infinite and indivisible, as did Parmenides in ancient Greece. Nor do we try to find a single basic stuff in water as Thales did, in air as Anaximenes did, in fire as Heraclitus did, in number as Pythagoras did. Increasingly, ours has become a world of the many, of plurality. We tend to think in terms of a field, of a configuration. The popular prefixes of our time are *"multi"* and *"poly,"* and we seem to hear less and less of the prefix *"mono."* Indeed, one is tempted to suggest that monorail and monogamy constitute a somewhat exhaustive list of words still in current good repute with the prefix "mono."

Many elements have combined to encourage the present pluralistic attitude. Our disenchantment with the authoritarian dogma of the Nazis and the Stalinists is a primary one. We have the literary expression of disillusionment in *The God That Failed*. A more philosophical statement is found in Karl Popper's *The Open Society and Its Enemies*. Literary dismay and philosophical analysis are rarely sufficient to effect a significant shift on the world scene. Monism, as a political, and quite possibly as a philosophical, orientation, received its death warrant when the American A-bomb fell on Japan. Henceforth there must be accommodation, and pluralism is the most likely position to afford this accommodation.

Other factors have been at work. Anthropological studies have given us cultural relativism. Ruth Benedict's *Patterns of Culture* is the high-water mark in this effort. Although we have grown less aggressive in promoting cultural relativism as the ultimate approach, we have been reluctant to return to the narrow, dogmatic notion that we have found the final, best culture. Linguistic science has suggested that language stands between man and reality; this has made us rather cautious in broadcasting to the world that our—whoever we may be—picture of reality is the correct one, to which all others must conform.

At the close of this chapter we shall return to a discussion of pluralism as a dominant concept in the contemporary world. For now, we need only remind ourselves that pluralism is "in the air," very much a part of our philosophic climate.

It is beyond the purpose of this chapter to assign values to the various factors that gave rise to pluralism. It seems simply apparent that the all too real encounters with Hitlerism and nuclear warfare have done more to put pluralism center stage than anything else. However, in the context of this chapter, it may be altogether appropriate to mention two forces in the United States that have played a significant part in the evolution of pluralism. These are the American experience as a developing nation and the pluralistic legacy of pragmatism.

Perhaps the most direct account of pluralism in American life has been given by John Herman Randall, Jr. He itemized four reasons why the American people are peculiarly devoted to pluralism.

The roots of this pluralistic attitude lie deep in American experience. There is, first, the fact that American thinkers have always been able to enjoy a certain perspective on the various cultures of Europe. They have been bound to no single intellectual tradition. . . . Secondly, the fact that America is a continent and not a nation has long led to an emphasis on "regionalism," on the wide differences between the various sections of our country. Thirdly, there is the deep-seated and traditional religious pluralism of American life. . . . Long accustomed to this diversity of faiths in the most important matters, Americans have found other diversities equally natural. Finally, there is the historical pluralism . . . fostered by the extraordinary rapid changes in American life.[1]

Randall continued his documentation by showing that the United States has never been a Hegelian state. Hegel was supreme in philosophic thought in academic America for a good many years. But for all of this, we never had much use for the Hegelian concept of the absolute state. Randall emphasized it thus:

For America is not a nation, but a continent. . . . It is not a nation; it is not bound together by those ties which European nations cherish—a common "stock," common traditions, a common religion. America, thank God, is united by no common and shared religion, to make it intolerant of other faiths and loyalties, as faith so often does. America has always been a welter of differing faiths, in which each has had to learn first to let others alone, then to respect them, and eventually to cooperate with them. Hence for Americans a man's "faith" has not been a "public" but a "private" matter—an attitude quite incomprehensible to Europeans, for whom "faith" has normally served as a club to enforce uniformity.[2]

Another commentator on American pluralism, Henry Steele Commager, has pointed out that we have been forced, as it were, into our pluralism because we were once thirteen states, then forty-eight, and now fifty. We could think of Americans as made up of regional, racial, and religious groups. In such a situation of multiplicity, "It would be all but fatal to insist on conformity to absolutes." [3] By and large, we have accepted the fact that we do not possess the whole truth, and this has been our good fortune. A society that possesses the whole truth "has no need for further truth, and properly silences those who submit unorthodox ideas." [4] According to Commager, if we have any system at all, it is the "habit of pluralism and experimentalism." [5]

Crane Brinton has described the nature of Western culture as "multanimity," by which he probably means pretty much the same characteristic that Randall and Commager mean by pluralism. We are multanimous, not unanimous, in our orientation.

A unanimous democracy—that is to say, a democratic society of millions of members all of whom were in agreement on the Big question—is almost inconceivable, and certainly in terms of the world we have grown up in, unlikely to intrude itself in the politics of our time. Certain societies in which men are agreed in such matters can be built in the mind; many, perhaps most, Utopias are based on this kind of agreement. . . .

In our time, at least, a democracy must be multanimous. This very definitely does not mean that in a democracy no one should really believe in God, or the life-force, or Science (with a capital S), or the single tax. . . .

It does mean that he must not kill them (those who believe otherwise), imprison them, close their gathering places; it does mean he must not hate them . . . it does mean, at bottom, that he must at least pay them sincerely the kind of respect he pays to the weather, or his wife, or anything else he knows he can't change. . . .

For the alternative to admitting that multanimity is, in our time at least, the normal state of a Western democracy, is to admit the increasing possibility of warfare, civil warfare, about ideas.[6]

Brinton observed that in any workable future, "some of our best friends will find beauty where we find ugliness, wisdom where we find folly, justice where we find injustice." [7] Brinton held this commitment to multanimity not to be a weakness but rather to be "one of our great strengths" in our struggle with Russia.[8] William G. Carleton, a political scientist, has written in much the same spirit:

When have the intellectuals of a single country of the Western world been united, let alone the intellectuals of the whole Western world? . . . The truth is that the Western world has never had intellectual unity, and it is too much to expect, with several kinds of revolutions— scientific, technological, economic, political, psychological—taking place in our midst, that we can achieve intellectual unity in the twentieth century.

The Western world can be true to itself only by clearly recognizing the inherent diversity and pluralism of its heritage, a diversity and pluralism which have been increasing century after century. . . . America's growing uniformity is essentially a betrayal of the American and of the Western heritage, and it is endangering the larger unity of the Western world.[9]

Although the United States may on occasion turn its back on this Western tradition of multanimity and pluralism, and although it may be more accurate to think of this tradition as an aspect of Western culture than as a private possession of the United States, it seems safe to hold that our experience with pluralism must be considered a major event of our history.

And pragmatism, the next force in the development of pluralism, has a special American touch. Wiener has assigned pluralism a high place in the philosophical legacy we have received from the founders of pragmatism. He wrote:

> First, it has an empirical respect for the complexity of existence requiring a plurality of concepts to do justice to the diverse problems of mankind. . . . Secondly, it has abandoned the eternal as an absolute frame of reference for thought and emphasized the ineluctable pervasiveness of temporal change. . . . Thirdly, it has regarded the nature of things, as known and appraised by men, to be relative to the categories and standards of the minds that have evolved modes of knowing and evaluating objects. Fourthly, it has insisted on the contingency and precariousness of the mind's interactions with the physical and social environment, so that in the most successful results of hard gained experimental knowledge, what we attain is fallible. Finally, American pragmatism upholds the democratic freedom of the individual inquirer and appraiser as an indispensable condition for progress in the future evolution of science and society.[10]

This summary of the legacy serves quite well to point up the importance of pluralism in the pragmatic tradition. A further comment from Wiener may help to demonstrate the pluralistic dimension basic to pragmatism. "Pluralistic empiricism is the piecemeal analysis of the diverse issues pertaining to physical, biological, psychological, linguistic, and social problems which resist resolution by a single metaphysical formula." [11]

It seems important to include here some remarks made by Ralph Barton Perry in 1912. They lend some historical depth to our discussion and provide another evaluation of the pluralistic content in pragmatism. Perry found absolutism to be "monistic, deterministic, quietistic," and pragmatism to be "pluralistic, indeterministic, melioristic." [12] Pluralism was seen as "the denial of absolute monism." "Absolute unity brooks no degrees; whereas pluralism demands no more than that you grant some separation among things . . . some real novelty." [13]

> Now if it is possible to know parts of reality without knowing all, it follows that such parts of reality are self-sufficient. If knowledge can be additive, if things can be known one at a time, then the things known must possess their natures independently. Thus we can know the laws of number, without knowing the date of Napoleon's birth. The latter knowledge, when obtained, is simply added to the former without modifying it. . . . It is not asserted that one is not related to the other, but only that it is not germane, does not enter into its definition. And this, when generalized, is what is meant by pluralism. According to the opposite, or monistic, view, the all-relationship, the relation of each to all, is definitive; according to pluralism, it is accidental. According to monism the universal interrelationship determines the essential nature of every item of being. . . . [14]

We have noted, then, that two aspects in the evolution of pluralism were the American experience as a developing nation, or perhaps the growth of the West as a civilization, and the pluralistic legacy of pragmatism. We might conclude that the pluralistic dimension of pragmatism was not as significant a contributing factor in the rise of pluralism as was the existence of a body of pluralistic philosophical work to which reference might be made. If one had an enforced pluralism, one would still lack any rationale by which to make sense of it. However, thanks to pragmatism, especially to William James, we were not caught philosophically dispossessed.

One hesitates to be dogmatic in an essay on pluralism, but at the time of this writing there can be no question: William James was *the* philosopher of pluralism. Paul Edwards and Arthur Pap selected James's essay "The Dilemma of Determinism" for their text, *A Modern Introduction to Philosophy,* 1957. Charles Frankel used the same essay for *The Golden Age of American Philosophy,* 1960. This essay first appeared in 1884. James was not without eloquence when he wrote of pluralism.

> The indeterminism I defend . . . gives us a pluralistic restless universe, in which no single point of view can ever take in the whole scene; and to a mind possessed of the love of unity at any cost, it will, no doubt, remain forever inacceptable. A friend with such a mind once told me that the thought of my universe made him sick, like the sight of the horrible motion of a mass of maggots in their carrion bed.
>
> But while I freely admit that the pluralism and the restlessness are repugnant and irrational in a certain way, I find that every alternative to them is irrational in a deeper way.
>
> Make as great an uproar about chance as you please, I know that chance means pluralism and nothing more.[15]

James was the poet laureate of pluralism, of the loose universe. No one has ever quite come up to him in this role. As he looked out at the "vast driftings of the cosmic weather," [16] he saw this pluralistic universe "in which no single point of view can ever take in the whole scene." [17] For him, philosophy, like life itself, "must keep the doors and windows open." [18] "Why should anywhere the world be absolutely fixed and finished?" [19]

James was an advocate of inclusiveness, by disposition and by temperament. Santayana wrote that "nobody ever recognized more heartily the chance that others had of being right, and the right they had to be different." [20] Perry saw the universe of James in these terms:

> His universe is a universe by virtue of its omitting nothing, by virtue of its indeterminate immensity and complexity, its unanalyzed ingredients, its unplumbed depths, its passage beyond every horizon, and not by virtue of any architecture, or structural delimitation, whether logical, aesthetic, or moral.[21]

James's universe could not be the "block universe." It had to be a universe with the lid off. He wrote: "The rationalist mind . . . is of a doctrinaire and authoritarian complexion: the phrase 'must be' is ever on its lips. The bellyband of its universe must be tight. A radical pragmatist on the other hand is a happy-go-lucky anarchistic sort of creature." [22]

To James, the choice between monism and pluralism was critical. "The difference between monism and pluralism is perhaps the most pregnant of all differences in philosophy." [23] James could not stand the monistic "glut of oneness." [24] "'The world is one!'—the formula may become a sort of number-worship. . . . Why is one more excellent than 43, or than two million and ten?" [25] "For monism the world is no collection, but one great all-inclusive fact outside of which is nothing— nothing is its only alternative." [26] James found it curious how little attention pluralism received from philosophers who were always busy "cleaning up the litter with which the world is apparently filled." [27]

In the 1930's Morris Cohen wrote: "I reject the euthanasia or suicide of thought involved in all monisms which identify the whole totality of things with matter, mind, or any other element in it." [28] In the 1950's Henry Myers wrote: " . . . The trend of modern philosophy has been gradually away from the classical conception of a single system and toward what may be called systematic pluralism." [29] This trend had its beginning largely with James. His battle against monism may be compared to Dewey's battle against dualism. James simply did not give up. Of monism he wrote: "The slightest suspicion of pluralism, the minutest wiggle of independence of any one of its parts from the control of the totality would ruin it. Absolute unity brooks no degrees." [30]

James found the following defects in monism:

1. It does not account for our finite consciousness. If nothing exists but as the Absolute Mind knows it, how can anything exist otherwise than as the Mind knows it?

2. It creates a problem of evil. . . . How, if Perfection be the source, should there be Imperfection?

3. It contradicts the character of reality as perceptually given. Of our world, change seems an essential ingredient.

4. It is fatalistic. . . . Monism rules out this whole conception of possibles.[31]

He assigned the following "great advantages" to pluralism:

1. It is more scientific.

2. It agrees more with the moral and dramatic expressiveness of life.

3. It is not obliged to stand for any particular amount of plurality, for it triumphs over monism if the smallest morsel of disconnectedness is once found undeniably to exist.[32]

But these formal attacks on monism do not represent James's great contribution to pluralism. What counts most for us are such bequests as his joy that there are real novelties in the world and his human philosophy which "stays inside the flux of life expectantly." [33] Here was a man who could hold that one must not love God too much. "When the love of God takes possession of . . . a mind, it expels all human loves and human uses." (James referred to this as a "theopathic condition.") [34] Here was a man who dared propose the "legitimacy of taking moral holidays."

John Passmore wrote, "James's pluralism . . . springs from his opposition to any suggestion that the individual human being is forced to act, or to believe, in one way rather than another because the 'scheme of things' leaves him no option." [35] David Riesman observed: "I myself feel that a certain looseness and disorderliness and variety of attitude are a part of the good life." [36] James seems to have understood the good life in these terms, and perhaps the crying need in these times is for more persons who can understand and enjoy the good life in this way.

Charles Peirce did not have much to say about pluralism. While his philosophy of fallibilism contained some implications for pluralism, he never assumed this stance with the vigor and gusto of James. John Dewey accepted pluralism, but again we do not find anything like the eloquence and dedication of James. In his essay on the development of American pragmatism, Dewey gave full credit to James's discussions of pluralism.

> [William James] shows that Monism is equivalent to a rigid universe where everything is fixed and immutably united to others, where indetermination, free choice, novelty, and the unforeseen in experience have no place; a universe which demands the sacrifice of the concrete and complex diversity of things to the simplicity and nobility of an architectural structure. In what concerns our beliefs, Monism demands a rationalistic temperament leading to a fixed and dogmatic attitude. Pluralism, on the other hand, leaves room for contingence, liberty, novelty, and gives complete liberty of action to the empirical method, which can be infinitely extended. It accepts unity where it finds it, but it does not attempt to force the vast diversity of events and things into a single rational mold.[37]

Later in the same essay, Dewey declared that a man who cherishes "novelty, risk, opportunity, and a variegated esthetic reality," will reject a belief in monism.[38] Elsewhere, Dewey rejected monism as dangerous in politics because it tends to glorify the state to the disadvantage of the individual. "Every combination of human forces that adds its own contribution of value to life has for that reason its own unique and ultimate worth." [39]

Dewey's quarrel with dualism and his Hegelian beginnings have recently brought him under suspicion of being a monist "at heart." Jacques Maritain made the accusation in rather guarded language.

> For he [John Dewey] certainly liberated himself from the Hegelian dialective, and from Hegelian idealism, and this

was the main thing. But he retained from Hegel the nostalgia for monism; the very notion of philosophy remained for him identified with the effort to absorb all things into one, and to eliminate, all the while respecting and maintaining the differences, every species of duality as well as every species of transcendence.[40]

It seems necessary to say here that although Dewey did wage unrelenting war on dualism and did not accept the realm of transcendence, he was in no sense a monist, for he had no use for the block universe, a universe with fixed values. Dewey's philosophy was pluralistic. He did not parade his pluralism the way James did—nor the way Schiller did.

It is in Schiller, rather than in Dewey, Peirce, or Mead, that we find the continuation of that pluralistic temperament so much a part of James, the man, and so much a part of James's philosophy. Schiller's open philosophy may well appear too open, even for some hearty pragmatists. He said, "I do not see why a humanist should not turn naturalist or supernaturalist upon occasion, when his human resources have left him in the lurch." [41] As far as Schiller was concerned, "there can probably be as many pragmatisms as there are pragmatists." [42]

In Schiller, we find again the loose universe of William James. Here again is a universe with the lid off. Schiller felt that men had cherished the absolute as a "guarantee against the contingency of experience." [43] He welcomed a universe "marred by chance." [44] Everything we know about reality indicates that it changes; and reality and truth are in a sense two sides of the same coin. Since reality is not a fixed piece of immutability, truth likewise is not fixed, but is forever changing.

All human truth, as it actually is and historically has been, seems fallible and transitory. It is of its nature to be liable to err, and of us to blind ourselves to this liability. The road to truth (if such a thing there is) grows indiscernible amid the many bypaths of error into which it branches off on either side, and whichever of these mazes men adopt, they plunge into it as gaily, follow it as faithfully, and trust it as implicitly, as if it were the one most certain highroad. But only for a season. For sooner or later they weary of a course that leads to nothing, and stop themselves with a shock of distressed surprise at the discovery that what they had so long taken to be true was really false. And yet so strong is the dogmatic confidence with which nature has endowed them, that they start again almost at once, all but a few of the wisest, upon the futile quest of a truth which in the end always eludes their human grasp.[45]

Schiller did not mean that men should give up the quest for truth but rather that they should ever continue the quest instead of resting on their oars in the belief that they had found it. It is this flux of reality and the incompleteness of the universe that allow us to go ahead with some confidence that we may be making progress. If we already had found absolute truth, then we should lose our freedom and whatever responsibility we might have as thinking beings. Schiller declared, "The notion of an absolute truth suggested itself as an expedient for escaping the continuous revaluation and transvaluation of truth."[46] As long as there is interaction between man and his environment, we cannot hope to realize the dreams of the absolutists, the hopes of the monists.

Absolute reality must in self-defense eschew all relations with ours. For such relations would involve a dependence on the imperfect which would disturb its own perfection. Relation among realities implies interaction, and interaction with the unstable and changing must import a reflected instability into the absolute reality and destroy its equipoise. The only way therefore for the perfect to preserve its perfection is to keep aloof: but if it does that, how, pray, shall it be known to us? [47]

The absolute is so at the mercy of accidental intrusions from an imperfect world that Schiller doubted if it were really worthwhile even as a temporary comfort stopover.

James wanted a universe where there were real losses, real risks, real adventure. In this respect he was much like Alfred North Whitehead, who held that the great ages were the unstable ones and that without adventure life and thought would be to no avail. It was here that Whitehead experienced difficulties with Dewey. Whitehead said: "You may have wondered at my coolness, not to John Dewey personally . . . but to his thought. The reason is that the emphasis of his thought is on security. But the vitality of a man's mind is in adventure." [48] Whitehead may not have referred to Schiller in his writings, but as to the adventure of the mind, the two of them, along with James, had much in common. Schiller took the position that the master passion of a rationalist, an absolutist, and a monist

. . . is not so much a love of reason as a fear of experience. I should define him, therefore, as essentially a person who will not trust experience, who wants at all costs to be insured against the risks, surprises, and novelties of life. . . . [49]

Schiller had no use for these "admirers of spick and span systems." [50] One could say of Schiller what Whitehead said of

James: "His intellectual life was one protest against the dismissal of experience in the interest of system." [51]

Profusion, said James, may be the keynote of reality. Schiller evinced the same spirit when he wrote of "the infinite and inexhaustible particularity of every act of thought." [52] Each thinker makes a unique contribution, and as soon as we admit individuals as significant participants in the thinking process, we have a toe in the door for an acceptance of pluralism. If truth comes from many persons, then truth itself may be many. On the other hand, the absolutist, according to Schiller,

> . . . simply cannot think of truth as many, as flexible, as relative to a plurality of persons and occasions, as varying with times and seasons, as changing and growing, as corrigible and improvable, as plastic and dynamic, as interesting and serving human interests and purposes and ministering to human life and human problems. He is merely puzzled, therefore, by the fact that in language "true" admits of a comparative and superlative, and so apparently, of less and more. [53]

We can have a plurality of truths because truth is situational and contextual, not in the sense of a relationship to some superhuman realm, but as related to concrete individual human beings.

Mathematics has been a great impetus for absolute concepts in philosophy. According to Whitehead, "Philosophy has been misled by the example of mathematics." [54] Bertrand Russell said he did not know of anyone who had been as influential in the field of thought as Pythagoras, because Pythagoras was a mathematician and as such, a primary influence on Platonic thought.

Mathematics is, I believe, the chief source of the belief in eternal and exact truth, as well as in a super-sensible intellectual world. Geometry deals with exact circles, but no sensible object is exactly circular; however carefully we may use our compasses, there will be some imperfections and irregularities. This suggests the view that exact reasoning applies to ideal as opposed to sensible objects; it is natural to go further, and to argue that thought is nobler than sense, and the objects of thought more real than those of sense-perception. Mystical doctrines as to the relation of time to eternity are also reinforced by pure mathematics, for mathematical objects, such as numbers, if real at all, are eternal and not in time. Such eternal objects can be conceived as God's thoughts. Hence Plato's doctrine that God is a geometer, and Sir James' belief that He is addicted to arithmetic.[55]

The long hand of Pythagoras, the mathematician, reaches down to our own day as philosophy. Somehow, the mathematical formulas of the analytical positivists, while no longer assumed to come from God, are often held to come from a realm not quite human.

Perhaps an examination of some of Schiller's thoughts on mathematics would prove helpful in furthering our pluralistic position in philosophy. Whitehead declared, "Exactness is a fake." [56] Fake or not, it has had, according to Schiller, "an uncanny fascination for the academic mind." [57] In response to a question as to what exactness means in mathematics, Schiller replied:

It clearly does not mean either that mathematical objects exactly reproduce realities or that physical realities exactly exemplify mathematical ideals. Straight lines and circles and units are not to be copied from nature, for they are not found in nature; while all the physical constants, like the year, the month, and the day are inexact and variable. In vain did astronomers postulate that heavenly bodies must move in perfect circles—in vain did they pile epicycle on epicycle to render astronomy an exact science; they have been forced by their own facts to admit that their laws and formulas were only conveniences of calculation. Now Plato had long ago recognized that there was no exactness to be found in the sensible world; yet he continued to think of God as a mathematician. He should have added that when "God geometrizes," he does so very inexactly.[58]

Mathematics may do all right as long as it remains mathematical. But as soon as it refers to objects of perception, it, too, becomes inexact. Its divine exactness prevails only so long as it operates in a mathematical vacuum. Schiller explained:

What is really meant by the exactness of mathematics is that mathematics is a science which can define its own objects, apparently without regard to reality. Mathematical truths primarily refer to ideal objects which the mathematician has himself created and defined. But in its relation to nature the mathematical ideal is a mere command, which may or may not apply. The rules of common arithmetic apply to a great variety of objects; but if we are wise we shall not expect four to result from the process of adding two drops of mercury to two others, or two lions to two lambs, or two to be the consequence of adding a bull to a cow. Nor should philosophers flatter themselves that definitions are revelations of the essence which makes all things what they are and utterly independent of empirical facts.[59]

According to Whitehead's illustration, "The togetherness of a spark and gunpowder produces an explosion, which is very unlike two things." [60]

Mathematics has to take cognizance of the contingencies of reality. It maintains its illusion of exactness by constantly revising itself. Schiller said:

> . . . In mathematics, as in every other science, knowledge grows and the definitions have to keep pace with this growth. As vehicles of growing knowledge they too must progressively change their meaning. If they are too stubborn and refuse to expand, they have to be scrapped.[61]

Schiller concluded that absolute exactness must be rejected as a useless fiction in mathematics.

It is possible that mathematics may afford us a good example of inexactness. "Indeed the process of stretching old definitions so as to permit of new operations is particularly evident in mathematics," [62] Schiller said. "The truth is that mathematical definitions cannot be more exact than our knowledge of the realities to which, sooner or later, directly or indirectly, they refer. Nor can mathematical symbols be more exact than words." [63] With all our use of mathematics today this last sentence must almost inevitably rub most of us the wrong way. There is scarcely any level of human experience so trivial that it has not been the subject of some statistical study. The distance between the refrigerator and the kitchen sink has been studied with the care once reserved for measuring such matters as the distance of the moon from Mars. But Schiller had a point. There comes a time when we leave our mathematical symbols and return to the use of ordinary words. "The abstract statement that two and two make four is always incomplete.

We need to know to what twos and fours the dictum is applied." [64]

It is rather ironic that at the very time when man is becoming sophisticated enough to put aside the prejudice favoring mathematics so imbedded in philosophy by Pythagoras and Plato, he finds himself in such a complex world that he must use mathematics on every hand in order to control his environment. The Greeks used mathematics to establish a meaningful relationship with the supernatural world, to look at essences that were God-made. We moderns use mathematics to survive amid the plethora of things we have created from matter. For all this new use of mathematics, we have not yet achieved a historical perspective on the use of mathematics as a metaphysical concept in past philosophical efforts. We recognize numbers as a measuring device of immense helpfulness in our world. With Schiller, we know it is not the "metaphysical essence of all things . . . but only a human device, a specifically human procedure." [65] But our philosophical heritage of mathematics as metaphysics has yet to be cleansed. We are as yet unemancipated from this heritage, and it is this heritage in part that makes for the heavy load of monistic, absolutistic philosophical nonsense that is still with us.

Schiller said he was not sure whether there were a priori truths, but he was dead sure that there were "a priori prejudices." One of these a priori prejudices—at least in his day—was the prejudice in favor of monism.

The rigidly monistic way of conceiving the universe is singularly unimaginative and lacking in variety. It cuts down the possibilities. . . . It shuts us off from infinite possibilities of things beautiful, good, and true, by the wanton dogmatism of its assumption that the absolute is already real, and that the attempt to remake it is as vain as it is blasphemous.

Consider, on the other hand, the advantages of discarding this notion. We can permit ourselves to recognise that reality is still in the making. Nothing is absolutely settled. Human operations are real experiments with a reality that really responds, and may respond differently to different manipulations.[66]

Surely, with the large increase in leisure we shall want an open plural universe that still is under construction. We shall need the possibilities both to keep from being bored to death or bombed to death.

Whitehead reminded us that tolerance could be "more often found with a genial orthodoxy." [67] Schiller seems to have possessed this genial orthodoxy, or perhaps we should simply call it a congenial philosophy. It is permissive. The duty of tolerance, Whitehead said, "is our finite homage to the abundance of inexhaustible novelty which is awaiting the future." [68]

Schiller refused to see either the present or the future as determined. "If the world is fully determined, there cannot be any alternatives." [69] Ethics becomes operational only in an indeterminate universe. The deficiency of determinism is "not merely that it fails to do full justice to the ethical fact of responsibility, but that it utterly annihilates the moral agent." [70]

As determinism works against responsibility, so the absolute truth works against democracy. The price tag on absolute truth is too high. Let us admit that we do not have absolute truth, "but that what we have is enough to content us. . . ." said Schiller. "Let us frame a new conception of Truth." [71] Democracy demands as much, since "every man has a vote in the making of truth." [72]

No man has a right to impose his convictions on any other; superior attractiveness alone effects conversion in the conflict of opinions. Nor has any one the right to argue that because he is right every one else must be wrong: Truth is plural, and can adjust herself to every man's sight and point of view. Hence an infinite variety of truths may be valid relatively to a variety of differently constituted and situated persons. Toleration mounts the throne left vacant by Infallibility.[73]

Let us work for human truths that will "no longer shine upon us from afar with the dim glimmer of an infinitely distant nebula." [74] Truths can be intimate, personal. But all of this carries an obligation. "Every man has an inalienable right to his opinion, to his personal reaction upon his world—until he can get a better. For the right to his opinion is the correlative of his duty to improve it." [75]

The purpose of this chapter so far has been to document pluralism as an integral part of pragmatism and to show that F. C. S. Schiller was second only to William James as an exponent of that pluralism. From the very start we have seen pluralism to be an essential dimension of pragmatism, and once more we find Schiller present as an eloquent spokesman for an aspect of pragmatism. He was no mere commentator; he was a founder.

The next step will be to show how pragmatic pluralism is relevant to the issues of the present. We have thoroughly and widely formulated pluralism as a theory in most areas of modern life, but we are still lacking in what one might call the pluralistic temperament. We theorize better than we feel.

Henry Adams took the position that the difficulties of education double with the coal output. But beyond the coal output, he saw a "next great influx of new forces." From 1200 to 1900 the movement from unity to multiplicity was "unbroken in sequence, and rapid in acceleration," he pointed out. "Prolonged one generation longer, it would require a new social mind." [76] It has now been prolonged, not one generation, but two generations—possibly three generations.

We seem to lack this "new social mind." We have had individual minds who could explain the relationship between education and the coal output, between education and the population explosion, nuclear warfare, and new communication media. Name a modern crisis, and you can name one or two or a dozen men who have been able to grasp rather well the implications of that crisis for mankind at large. What we lack is the *social* mind that can feel at home among these forces and exercise effective control over them. It is not that there is a sharp antithesis between the individual mind and the social mind; it is not that there is a sharp antithesis between mind and feeling; but it remains that we have not gotten around to feeling comfortable with this influx of new forces.

Karl Popper has explained the dangers of historicism—long-range social prophecy, the sacred blueprint for the future. He has shown us the folly of following the dedicated utopians who would lead us onward to an earthly El Dorado.

> The Utopian engineer . . . is convinced that we must recast the whole structure of society, when we experiment with it; and he can therefore conceive a more *modest* experiment only as one that recasts the whole structure of a *small* society. . . . The Utopian method must lead to a dangerous dogmatic attachment to a blueprint for which countless sacrifices have been made. Powerful interests must become linked up with the success of the experiment. All this does not contribute to the rationality, or to the scientific value, of the experiment. But the piecemeal

method permits repeated experiments and continuous readjustments. In fact, it might lead to the happy situation where politicians begin to look out for their own mistakes instead of trying to explain them away and to prove that they have always been right.

. . . It is said that the social scientist or philosopher has to survey things from a higher plane. He sees the individual as a pawn, as a somewhat insignificant instrument in the general development of mankind. And he finds that the really important actors on the Stage of History are either the Great Nations and their Great Leaders, or perhaps the Great Classes, or the Great Ideas. . . . He will try to understand the laws of historical development. . . .

This is a brief description of an attitude which I call *historicism*.[77]

Popper has held that "measures should be planned to fight concrete evils rather than to establish some ideal good." [78] He has warned that "the attempt to make heaven on earth invariably produces hell." [79] Albert Camus has been a bit more specific.

In the Marxian perspective, a hundred thousand corpses are nothing if they are the price of the happiness of hundreds of millions of men. But the sure death of millions of men for the hypothetical happiness of the survivors seems too high a price to pay. The dizzy rate at which weapons have evolved, a historical fact ignored by Marx, forces us to raise anew the whole question of means and ends. And in this instance, the means can leave us little doubt about the end. Whatever the desired end, however lofty and necessary, whether happiness or justice or liberty—the means employed to attain it represent so enormous a risk and are so disproportionate to the slender hopes of success, that, in all sober objectivity, we must refuse to run this risk.[80]

Camus and Popper have both appealed for the Open Society, or what Camus called "the relative Utopia."

While Popper's book is a long scholarly work, most of us can get the message: we do not want great misery in the present as the intolerable means by which to realize distant, dreamy Utopian ends. We are committed to "piecemeal social experiments" that represent a pluralistic approach, and we would avoid grand blueprints for the great future that represent a monistic authoritarian approach.

This much we seem to grasp.

But if we shift our attention from the open society, the macrocosm, to the open individual, the microcosm, we may feel less at ease. Earl Kelley has given us a picture of the open self.

That which is needed as a screen or filter to protect the individual from the miscellaneous bombardment of externality has a tendency to become too thick and hard, so that very little can get through it. It becomes an isolating wall, so that the organism is deprived of much that would enhance it, if it could get in. Words bounce off this wall, unless the words express ideas in keeping with the individual's already established attitudes and prejudices. . . .

The worst feature of the development of these walls of isolation is that they deprive the individual of one of his most basic needs—other people. . . . We need to do what we can to bring about the education of the open self in all people.[81]

A world of open selves is pluralistic; a world of closed selves is conformist.

Pluralism may be the developmental manner of nations and civilizations; it may also be the method by which nations and civilizations relate themselves to other nations and civilizations. William G. Carleton has written that today "not monolithism but pluralism is the dominant trend in the world." [82] If we can believe George F. Kennan,[83] we are seeing "polycentrism" substituted for the two-world concept of East and West. Within the Communist bloc we have many power centers; and the same holds true for us in the West.

Louis J. Halle has taken much the same position. "For an indefinite future, the society of mankind will be a pluralistic society, a society that can exist only by tolerating and accommodating diversity in its constituent parts." [84] But this is only one aspect of our contemporary pluralism. "A good American society will not, ultimately, exist apart from a good world society. This means that it must be a society based on the tolerance of diversity—the tolerance of diversity inside its borders as well as outside." [85]

In a sense, political units have a certain accommodation forced upon them, unless they want to fight to the death of the last soldier in their armies. On the whole, religions have been able to maintain a more uncompromising attitude than national states. Yet at this stage in history, there is good reason to believe that the shift toward pluralism is more pronounced in religion than in politics. There has been a growing religious tolerance among faiths that has been taking place beyond the church door and the religious conference. Max Lerner has commented:

> The sects have been derided because they split what might have been religious unity and cast themselves out of the "Eden of infallibility." Yet to attack them for this is to ask America to be other than it is, not only in religion but

in every phase of its life. For the pluralism of the American churches is like the pluralism of America's regions, its diverse economic forms, its political localism, its ethnic and immigrant stocks.[86]

This is an adopted pluralism, a pluralism that grows out of the American experience of being a melting pot that never quite melted.

Another index to religious pluralism is the Supreme Court's decision on public school prayer. More and more, the minor sect has had its rights protected. More and more, the heretic, even the atheist, has found his rights protected. One is tempted to change Will Herberg's title to read *Protestant–Catholic–Jew–Atheist*.

But more important, perhaps, than this external religious pluralism that has been coming to religion from our political structure is what we may call an internal religious pluralism. We are beginning to see religious liberty as a religious right, not a political right. The deliberations of the Vatican Council surely constitute an important event in this phase of religious pluralism. We have seen articles in religious journals by the clergy suggesting an accommodation with atheists—if not with atheism.

A professor of theology has written that the Christian must henceforth "recognize that his faith is one among many and that it cannot be set over against all other human phenomena as that one point at which God has acted." [87] The same theologian, a Protestant, looks upon the work of the Catholic Teilhard de Chardin as "defining nothing on the ground that 'it is written' or that 'it is Christian,' avidly open to all truth—yet still *believing*. This mood is one with which I can identify myself as theologian, as Christian, as man." [88]

Another aspect of religious pluralism would be the religious syncretism as we find it in Arnold Toynbee. Although Toynbee has been held up as the intellectuals' Billy Graham, as the scholar who bases the future of civilization on the higher religion known as Christianity, a closer reading of Toynbee is enough to send shivers all over a Christian with a monistic disposition.

> The fundamental positive motive for toleration is a recognition of the truth that religious conflict is not just a nuisance but a sin. It is sinful because it arouses the wild beast in Human Nature. Religious persecution, too, is sinful because no one has a right to try to stand between another human soul and God. . . . Different people's convictions will differ, because Absolute Reality is a mystery of which no more than a fraction has ever yet been penetrated by—or revealed to—any human mind. The heart of so great a mystery cannot ever be reached by following one road only.[89]

To Toynbee, self-centeredness is a sin, and the worst kind of self-centeredness is religious. We are moving. In religion, "it is a difficult time for monoliths." [90]

When we find pluralists operating freely and openly in the field of religion, we should not be surprised to find pluralism in metaphysics. Myers has described pluralism as

> the metaphysical theory that reality is known through a number, potentially infinite, of systems of knowledge. Each of these systems reveals the essence of reality *from its point of view,* which is determined by its categories. . . . There can be no ultimate system, for each new system must like all others be limited by its categories and hence must take its place in an infinite series.[91]

We need new ways to consider reality; perhaps we are getting them. In any event, we are being invited to assume a pluralistic approach to reality. Louis Arnaud Reid has written:

> But whatever is true of the physicists' world, it is beyond any doubt that the reality both made and revealed by art is an expanding reality. Music, for instance, is certainly not representing the given "real." But it is revealing new reality in new creation—continuous creation—and its universe is always expanding. . . .
>
> Why should we limit "reality" to what the plain matter of fact man assumes it to be—ready-made and complete, what common sense and science can show? This assumption underlies the naive conception of truth—of a world of solid substantial reality, to which the insubstantial fabrications of the mind have to conform, to which they must submit. But this is far too shallow.[92]

Perhaps we have been overstating the case for pluralism. Gabriel Vahanian, a theologian, has said that "pluralism can only be an interlude." [93] While it is not the province of this book to argue whether or not pluralism is only an interlude in religion, we may at least observe that the religion or religions to which we return after our interlude of pluralism will be much different from our pre-interlude religions.

It would be possible to pose the problem in a contrary way—that when one considers the number of religions and of philosophies that have come and gone, it becomes possible to assume that pluralism is the normal condition, while all faiths and philosophies appear only as interludes. But we need not push our thinking in that direction. We need simply hold that for us in the second half of the twentieth century, pluralism is more than an interlude. It is by necessity and by choice our metaphysical position.

CARL A. RUDISILL LIBRARY
LENOIR RHYNE COLLEGE

Yet there remains a deficiency: although pluralism may be our particular metaphysics, we have not developed a gusto for living as pluralists. We still lack the pluralistic temperament to go with our pluralism. James and Schiller are so important because they loved their pluralism and took great joy in it. It may well be that in order to feel at home with our pluralism, we can do no better than to turn to William James and F. C. S. Schiller.

1. John Herman Randall, Jr., "The Spirit of American Philosophy," in F. Ernest Johnson (ed.), *Wellsprings of the American Spirit* (New York: Harper & Bros., 1948), p. 126.

2. *Ibid.*, p. 122.

3. Henry Steele Commager, *Freedom, Loyalty, Dissent* (New York: Oxford University Press, 1954), p. 67.

4. *Ibid.*, p. 58.

5. *Ibid.*, p. 69.

6. Crane Brinton, *The Shaping of the Modern Mind* (New York: New American Library, 1953), pp. 14–17.

7. *Ibid.*, p. 14.

8. *Ibid.*, p. 13.

9. William G. Carleton, "An Atlantic Curtain." Reprinted from THE AMERICAN SCHOLAR, Vol. XXII, No. 3, Summer, 1953. Copyright © 1953, by the United Chapters of Phi Beta Kappa. By permission of the publishers.

10. Philip P. Wiener, *Evolution and the Founders of Pragmatism* (Cambridge: Harvard University Press, 1949), p. 191.

11. *Ibid.*, p. 191.

12. Ralph Barton Perry, *Present Philosophical Tendencies* © New York: George Braziller, 1955), p. 199.

13. *Ibid.*, p. 373.

14. *Ibid.*, p. 243.

15. Charles Frankel (ed.), *The Golden Age of American Philosophy*, pp. 160–61.

16. *Pragmatism,* p. 105.

17. *The Will to Believe,* p. 177.

18. William James, *Some Problems of Philosophy* (New York: Longmans, Green & Co., 1911), p. 100.

19. *The Meaning of Truth,* p. 92.

20. George Santayana quoted in Ralph Barton Perry, *The Spirit of William James* (New Haven: Yale University Press, 1938), p. 150.

21. *Ibid.,* p. 107.

22. *Pragmatism,* p. 259.

23. James, *The Will to Believe,* p. vii.

24. James, *Pragmatism,* p. 150.

25. *Ibid.,* p. 132.

26. William James, *A Pluralistic Universe* (New York: Longmans, Green & Co., 1909), p. 36.

27. *Ibid.,* p. 45.

28. Morris R. Cohen, *Reason and Nature* (Glencoe, Ill.: Free Press, 1953), p. xiii.

29. Henry Alonzo Myers, *Systematic Pluralism* (Ithaca: Cornell University Press, 1961), p. 7.

30. *Pragmatism,* p. 160.

31. *Some Problems of Philosophy,* pp. 130–40.

32. *Ibid.,* pp. 142–43.

33. *Ibid.,* p. 100.

34. *The Varieties of Religious Experience,* p. 267.

35. *A Hundred Years of Philosophy,* p. 109.

36. David Riesman, *Individualism Reconsidered* (Glencoe, Ill.: Free Press, 1954), p. 164.

37. *Philosophy and Civilization,* pp. 19–20.

38. *Ibid.,* p. 21.

39. *Reconstruction in Philosophy,* p. 159.

40. Jacques Maritain, *Moral Philosophy* (New York: Chas. Scribner's Sons, 1964), p. 400.

41. *Our Human Truths,* p. 20.

42. *Ibid.*, pp. 78–79.

43. F. C. S. Schiller, *Studies in Humanism* (London: Macmillan Co., 1907), p. 255. All quotations from this work are used by permission of Macmillan & Co., Ltd., London.

44. *Ibid.*, p. 469.

45. *Ibid.*, p. 205.

46. *Ibid.*, p. 206.

47. *Ibid.*, p. 216.

48. Lucien Price, *Dialogues of Alfred North Whitehead* (Boston: Little, Brown & Co., 1954), p. 255.

49. Schiller, *Studies in Humanism*, p. 255.

50. Schiller, *Riddles of the Sphinx*, p. 4.

51. Alfred North Whitehead, *Modes of Thought* (New York: Capricorn Books, 1958), p. 4.

52. *Our Human Truths*, p. 293.

53. *Ibid.*, p. 50.

54. Alfred North Whitehead, *Process and Reality* (New York: Macmillan Co., 1929), p. 12.

55. *A History of Western Philosophy*, p. 37. Copyright © 1945 by Bertrand Russell.

56. Paul A. Schilpp (ed.), *The Philosophy of Alfred North Whitehead* (New York: Tudor Publishing Co., 1951), pp. 113, 700.

57. *Our Human Truths*, p. 305.

58. *Ibid.*, pp. 305–6.

59. *Ibid.*, p. 306.

60. Schilpp, *op. cit.*, p. 199.

61. *Our Human Truths*, p. 306.

62. *Ibid.*, p. 341.

63. *Ibid.*, p. 341.

64. Schiller, *Studies in Humanism*, p. 9.

65. Schiller, *Our Human Truths*, pp. 29–30.

66. Schiller, *Studies in Humanism*, p. 218.

67. Alfred North Whitehead, *Adventures of Ideas* (Cambridge: Cambridge University Press, 1933), p. 63.

68. *Ibid.*, p. 65.

69. F. C. S. Schiller, "Choice," *Hibbert Journal,* July, 1909, p. 805.

70. *Ibid.*, p. 806.

71. F. C. S. Schiller, "Infallibility and Tolerance," *Hibbert Journal,* April, 1909, pp. 81–82.

72. *Ibid.*, p. 84.

73. *Ibid.*, p. 84.

74. *Ibid.*, p. 83.

75. F. C. S. Schiller, "William James and the Making of Pragmatism," in Daniel Sommer Robinson (ed.), *An Anthology of Recent Philosophy* (New York: Thomas Y. Crowell Co., 1929), pp. 259–260.

76. Henry Adams, *The Education of Henry Adams* (New York: Modern Library, 1931), p. 498.

77. Karl L. Popper, *The Open Society and Its Enemies* (Princeton: Princeton University Press, 1950), pp. 159–60.

78. *Ibid.*, p. 320.

79. *Ibid.*, p. 422.

80. Albert Camus, "Neither Victims nor Executioners," *Liberation,* February, 1960, p. 8.

81. Earl C. Kelley, "Communication and the Open Self." Reprinted by permission from *ETC: A Review of General Semantics,* Vol. XI, No. 2; copyright, 1954, by the International Society for General Semantics.

82. William G. Carleton, "Our Post-Crisis World." Reprinted from THE AMERICAN SCHOLAR, Vol. XXXIII, No. 1, Winter, 1963–64. Copyright ©, 1964, by the United Chapters of Phi Beta Kappa. By permission of the publishers.

83. George F. Kennan, "Polycentrism and Western Policy," *Foreign Affairs,* January, 1964.

84. Louis J. Halle, "The World: A Sense of History," *New Republic,* November 7, 1964, p. 107.

85. *Ibid.*, p. 107.

86. Max Lerner, *America As a Civilization* (New York: Simon & Schuster, 1957), p. 711.

87. John B. Cobb, Jr., "From Crisis Theology to the Post-Modern World," *Centennial Review,* Spring, 1964, p. 178.

88. *Ibid.,* p. 181.

89. Arnold Toynbee, *An Historian's Approach to Religion* (New York: Oxford University Press, 1956), pp. 252–53.

90. Harvey Cox, "Facing the Secular," *Commonweal,* February 21, 1964, p. 619.

91. Myers, *op. cit.,* p. 181.

92. Louis Arnaud Reid, "Art, Truth, and Reality," *British Journal of Aesthetics,* October, 1964, pp. 330–31.

93. Gabriel Vahanian, "The Future of Christianity in a Post-Christian Era," *Centennial Review,* Spring, 1964, p. 171.

V. Schiller's Philosophy as Subjectivism

Two sentences from the nineteenth century haunt twentieth-century man. The first comes from Dostoevsky: *If God did not exist, everything would be permitted.* The second comes from Nietzsche: *God is dead.* These two statements have been the starting point for a great deal of atheistic existential thought as well as for a great deal of theistic theological thought. For a long time, man comforted himself with belief in a transcendent reality. It was "out there," and it was independent of mankind. God was there as an objective fact. The good, the true, and the beautiful could be grounded in God. One had only to think in terms of the ladder of perfection to put each thing in its rightful place, from the lowly amoeba to the man of genius. Since Nietzsche spoke, a certain simplicity of thought has departed. Some have retreated, for, as Camus said, "nostalgia is stronger than knowledge." [1] Others have engaged in radical theologizing, as did Tillich. Some, like Sartre, have rejoiced that now man is responsible for what he is and what he will become.

When the firm, objective anchorage of God appeared to be

in some jeopardy, man placed new demands on his sciences. If divine transcendence was not an objective fact, then perhaps we could find a substitute in the objective knowledge of science. Here again, it was feared that if objectivity did not exist, everything would be permitted. If man, and man alone, was the measure of all things, then we would experience unlimited anarchy. So we heard much about natural law; the neo-conservatives discovered a firm anchorage in Edmund Burke; some leftists secured themselves with the dialectics of Marx; and there was talk about a value-free science, which was sometimes called pure science.

Walter Lippmann, seeing things getting rather out of hand, made a plea for a "public philosophy," with certain reservations, such as "There are limits beyond which we cannot carry the time-honored method of accommodating the diversity of beliefs." [2] Lippmann brought together the theologian and the scientist in his entreaty.

> The crucial point, however, is not where the naturalists and supernaturalists disagreed. It is that they did agree that there was a valid law which, whether it was the commandment of God or the reason of things, was transcendent. They did agree that it was not something decided upon by certain men and then proclaimed by them. It was not someone's fancy, someone's prejudice, someone's wish or rationalization, a psychological experience and no more. It is there objectively, not subjectively. It can be discovered. It has to be obeyed. [3]

"The critical question" became whether man could "experience a reality absolutely independent of himself." [4] Lippmann saw Sartre as having done away with both God and "the recognition that beyond our private worlds there is a public world to which we belong." [5] He also rejected those theologians who taught "that religious experience is a purely psychological phenomenon, related to nothing beyond each man's psychic condition." [6]

It appeared that Lippmann would impose his public philosophy on the people by some variation of Plato's philosopher-king. The people were to be saved once more from on high and were not considered quite equal to saving themselves. There had to be this something—this "reality absolutely independent of man."

But maybe we cannot have this consummate objectivity. One would not, at first thought, expect to find the defense of subjectivity in the work of a physicist. Yet, perhaps, our most eloquent refutation of transcendence, whether natural or supernatural, occurred in the work of P. W. Bridgman, a Nobel Prize winner in physics.

Not only do I see that I cannot get away from myself, but I see that you cannot get away from yourself. The problem of how to deal with the insight that we never get away from ourselves is perhaps the most important problem. . . .

Not only is each one of us as an individual not able to get away from himself, but the human race as a whole can never get away from itself. The insight that we can never get away from ourselves is an insight which the human race through its long history has been deliberately, one is tempted to say willfully, refusing to admit. But the ostensibly timeless absolutes are formulated and apprehended by us, and the vision which the mystic says is revealed by the direct intervention of God is still a vision apprehended by him. When we talk about getting away from ourselves it is we who are talking. All this is so obvious that it has only to be said, yet it seems to me to have been a major concern of most conventional philosophy and religion to sidestep the consequences of this insight, or not to admit it in the first place.[7]

Bridgman called it "the merest truism that all our experimental understanding is impossible and non-existent apart from our mental processes," and that "the nature of our thinking mechanism essentially colors any picture that we can form of nature." [8]

We are inclined to associate subjectivity with art and literature, and in these areas we tend to praise the subjective and question the objective. But Bridgman extended the subjective to "pure physics," where it was becoming evident "that the problem of 'observer' must eventually deal with the observer as thinking about what he observes." [9] Or again: "Processes of verification do not occur in nature apart from human beings." Bridgman went on to say that a computer does not malfunction from the point of view of a computer but rather from the point of view of some man.[10]

Yet the possibility of pure and absolute objectivity forever fascinates man. Henry Adams observed: "No honest historian can take part with—or against—the forces he has to study. To him even the extinction of the human race should be merely one fact to be grouped with other vital statistics." [11] Frederick Breed warned that if there were no independent reality, man would take on a quixotic sense of power. He told us that "with the exaggeration of human power goes the flattery of human hopes. . . . The world that man has made, he can quite easily unmake." [12] This was Bertrand Russell's objection to the philosophy of John Dewey.

> His philosophy is a power philosophy, though not like Nietzsche's, a philosophy of individual power; it is the

power of the community that is felt to be powerful. It is this element of social power that seems to me to make the philosophy of instrumentalism attractive to those who are more impressed by our new control over natural forces than by the limitations to which that control is still subject.

The attitude of man towards the non-human environment has differed profoundly at different times. The Greeks . . . carefully avoided what would have seemed to them an insolence towards the universe. The Middle Ages carried submission much further: . . . Man, formerly too humble, begins to think of himself as almost a God. The Italian pragmatist Papini urges us to substitute the "Imitation of God" for the "Imitation of Christ."

In all this I feel a grave danger, the danger of what might be called cosmic impiety. The concept of "truth" as something dependent upon facts largely outside of human control has been one of the ways in which philosophy hitherto has inculcated the necessary element of humility. When this check upon pride is removed, a further step is taken on the road towards a certain kind of madness—the intoxication of power. . . .[13]

Dewey never really seemed intoxicated with power, but that was not the major issue bothering Russell in the above comment.

We are dealing here with fundamental issues in philosophy, with unresolved problems in morality, epistemology, and other areas. Without God, everything is permitted. Without virtue, everything is permitted. Without truth, everything is permitted. And without independent objective reality, everything is permitted.

If we must assign pragmatism a place in this objective-subjective dispute, we may align it with subjectivism. There it can avoid the dilemma of idealism, which is usually committed to some transcendent idea, and the dilemma of realism, which is usually committed to some variation of the independent reality concept. It seems that pragmatism got off to a fine start in the way it came to grips with this problem. From the very beginning, it espoused the scientific method and the importance of the individual person. It was a form of personalism supported by the scientific method and the democratic process. It began by stressing process and not substance. Our present concern is with the subjectivism we find in pragmatism during its early days.

To document the case for subjectivism in the formulation of pragmatism, we can turn first to C. S. Peirce, the representative of the analytical dimension in pragmatism. He was what William Earle called the technical philosopher: the philosopher who would professionalize wisdom, who worried excessively about the general muddleheadedness of other philosophers, who was quite mathematical in his approach, and who wanted to remain "invisible behind his symbols." [14] Peirce had a laboratory mind.

It was Peirce who announced the subjective element in pragmatism. To James, he wrote: "You and Schiller carry pragmatism too far for me." [15] Dewey was guilty of "intellectual licentiousness," [16] while "I, by no means, follow Mr. Schiller's brilliant and seductive humanistic logic, according to which it is proper to take account of the whole personal situation in logical inquiries." He referred to this aspect of Schiller's philosophy as "Mr. Schiller's charming lane." [17] In each instance, to a greater or lesser degree, Peirce was complaining about the subjective factors connected with the work of these three associates in pragmatism.

It hardly seems necessary to discuss the subjective qualities of the philosophy of William James. We are well aware of the place he assigned to personal temperament as an active

ingredient in any man's philosophy. We know of the great significance he attributed to "the world of concrete personal experiences." His will to believe was an important part of his
personalism.

Our major concern is Schiller. There is a highly personalistic or subjectivist character in his metaphysics, his concept of
truth and his view of logic.

Schiller had his misgivings about metaphysics, but like a
good pragmatist, he said it ought to be useful. Metaphysics
would not be "valued any longer because of the magniloquent
obscurity with which it speaks of unfathomable mysteries
which have no real concern with human life, or because it
paints fancy pictures which mean nothing to any but their
painters." Instead, it would "henceforth have to test all its
assumptions by their working." [18] But too often, it fell short of
this goal of working. The metaphysician was not guided by
very practical goals.

> The metaphysician wings in his flight to the invisible, and
> loses sight of the earth altogether. He closes his eyes and
> hardens his heart to the facts of life. He declares unreal
> whatever does not fit into the narrow limits of his theories,
> on the ground that whatever is real is rational, and leaving
> to his disciples a glittering legacy of magniloquent but
> unmeaning phrases, he vanishes into the air before he is
> caught and questioned about the meanings of his enchant-
> ments.[19]

Metaphysics only became dangerous because of "the preposter-
ous pretensions" made in its behalf. Schiller, for all his worries
about this discipline, was still having a go at it in his last book.

> Metaphysics is the name for the loftiest and most ar-
> duous region of the philosophic field, which promises its

votaries the finest views and an all-embracing conception of the whole. It has, however, drawbacks too. Its peaks are plentiful and are suspected to be virgin; for the more accounts of their alleged ascents one reads the more doubtful one grows whether anyone has ever really climbed to their very tops. Moreover, they are nearly always shrouded in thick clouds and impenetrable fog, the ascent to them is steep, and the going rough; while the atmosphere on the summits must be so highly rarefied that no one could maintain himself at that altitude for long. So it is no wonder that metaphysicians are rare and precious and that metaphysical ascents are not adventures for the masses but fit only for the trained and hardy few, with the best guides. They are, indeed, a form of intellectual mountaineering.[20]

In his own metaphysical speculations Schiller escaped from all the pomposity and rarefied air. Schiller made metaphysics readable, even fun—no mean achievement.

Schiller's metaphysics was of the self, from his earliest writings to his last. He found the personal self beneath the metaphysical façade. He wrote in 1912:

The proposed aim of metaphysics is to synthesize all knowledge, to systematize the data of the sciences, and to reflect on the universe as a whole. But this lofty ambition necessarily renders it intensely personal. . . . Practically, therefore, a system of metaphysics, with whatever pretensions to pure thought and absolute rationality it may start, is always in the end one man's personal vision about the universe, and the "metaphysical craving," often so strong in the young, is nothing but the desire to tell the universe what one thinks of it.[21]

For Schiller, this metaphysical craving, which some would have us believe is an effort to escape from the self to some disembodied heaven of pure impersonal abstractions, was really nothing of the sort. It was self-bound. The self was his starting point in metaphysics, and inescapable. The self should be "taken quite seriously as a real agent. . . . All experience is relative to a self, all acts of knowledge are performed by selves." [22]

And since metaphysics professes to be an all-embracing effort, it is therefore a personal effort.

> If it is the duty of metaphysics to leave out nothing, . . . to aspire to the whole of experience, it must have this personal tinge. For a man's personal life must contribute largely to his data, and his idiosyncrasy must colour and pervade whatever he experiences. It is surely the most sinister and fatal of abstractions to abstract from the variety of individual minds, in order to postulate a universal substance in which the personal is obliterated, because you are too ignorant or indolent to cope with its exuberance.[23]

Schiller said that the final form of any metaphysics would be that of an idiosyncrasy. "A metaphysic which is true for one man, because it seems to him to synthesize his experiences, may be false to another, because his personality is different." [24] A genuine metaphysics becomes "the most individual thing in the world." The only way we can make sense out of the endless varieties of philosophies is to see them as "the expressions of their makers." He concluded, "The whole history of philosophy thus becomes an eloquent paean on the triumph of personality." [25]

Schiller's views on truth expressed a similar emphasis on the importance of the self. Again, he was not pleased by the way truth had been treated by philosophers. In fact, he was not sure that they had been interested in truth. He found that "one of Plato's noblest lies proclaimed the doctrine that philosophers are lovers of truth." [26] If we are to make much headway, we must proceed largely unencumbered by earlier approaches to the truth. "Of all the philosophic questions that of truth is perhaps the most hackneyed and unanswerable when treated in the usual way." One of the usual ways is to engage in "ecstatic rhapsodies about the sacredness of truth." [27]

Schiller was not given to extolling the sacredness of truth, but stressed its very human quality. "It must be frankly admitted that *truth is human truth,* and incapable of coming into being without human effort and agency." [28] Instead of all sorts of fanciful flights to discover some objective basis for truth, he suggested "a thoroughly and consistently dependent truth, dependent, that is, on human life and ministering to its needs, made by us and referring to our experience, and evolving everything called real and absolute and transcendent." [29] He advised that we stay with ourselves. "For why should anyone wish to make unverifiable assertions about the unknowable? What does it matter what is done or suffered by a Real which is out of relation to us?" [30] He said that we want to know what a particular reality is in relation to us.

To Schiller, truth was contextual. "Nothing more is required of a truth than that it should be relevant to a specific situation." [31] And truth, for him, was related to a purpose. True meant true for someone for some purpose. Another characteristic of truth, for Schiller, was usefulness. That "truth works" has been a bugaboo in the history of pragmatism. It is perhaps too bad that James ever said anything about the cash value of an idea. But in the best sense of these criteria, Schiller held firmly to standards of usefulness and workability. He contended that "usefulness is no presumption of untruth, but rather the reverse." [32] "We need principles that work, not principles that possess testimonials from the highest of a priori quarters." [33] " . . . If our knowledge works it is true in the only sense which truth can bear." [34]

Schiller proposed that we think of truth as something that has been made. "All truth must, methodologically, be treated as if it had been made." [35] His idea was that a truth that has been made is a truth that can be improved. "But if our concepts are immutable, our knowledge cannot grow," he pointed out. "And conversely, if our knowledge grows, our concepts cannot be immutable." [36]

The subjective content in James's and Schiller's concept of truth has alienated many a philosopher. This antagonism did not stop Schiller, for he moved his personalism beyond philosophy and into the field of science itself.

> The sciences . . . all try to depersonalize themselves and to present a show of impersonal truths about objective fact. It is only when we pry into their genesis and history that we perceive how deceptive this appearance is. It is only then that we realize how ephemeral scientific truths are. . . . They are all at the outset personal affairs. They are launched upon the scientific world by the personal observations, exertions, experiences, and experiments of those who sponsored them, and arose in a context of particular times and places.[37]

To Schiller, the idea of a depersonalized and inhuman science was a fairy tale. He said that "the abstraction from personality, which was supposed to be characteristic of scientific method, had long been known to be a fiction . . . astronomy had long been forced to allow for the 'personal equation' of its observers." [38]

Turn where you will, in the work of Schiller there is personality. It resembles not a mirror but rather the "atmosphere through which is seen whatever we see. . . . In no case is it possible to get rid of personality." [39]

Schiller's contributions to the field of logic may be found throughout his writings. His two major contributions to logic are "Axioms as Postulates," an essay that appeared in 1902, and *Logic for Use,* a book published in 1930. A reviewer in the *New Republic* said of the book: "He emphasizes the personal and subjective aspects of knowledge and understanding. He is anxious to strip away every pretension that formal logic has to objectivity, usefulness, and truth, and to put in its place a voluntaristic logic." [40] The reviewer may have gone a little far, but what he said indicates the nature of Schiller's logic. It is personal, subjective, and begins with man. "There is no thought without a thinker, no observation without an observer, not even a dream without a dreamer, and no object without a subject." [41] And again: " . . . Our thinking is volitional through and through." [42]

Pragmatism has been beset by a number of expressions that have worked to the detriment of an understanding of it. They have given its enemies grist for their mill. One of them is Dewey's: "Education is growth." Another is James's: "The will to believe." The message evidently strikes many as so obvious that they feel no need to explore the implications of these brief phrases. Schiller's counterpart to James's thesis of the "will to believe" is found in "Axioms as Postulates." A careful reading of this essay would do much to recondition the interpretation many have placed too facilely upon James's expression. The "right to postulate" was Schiller's way of stating James's proposition: we must believe in order to act; that is, we make postulates or assumptions in order to act. A postulate is simply an indication of an "intelligent purposive volition." [43]

Schiller said: "The organism cannot help postulating . . . because it must act or die. . . . It therefore needs assumptions it can act on and live by." [44] Frequently, we cannot delay acting simply because we lack evidence for an act. We make up for the lack of evidence through the processes of will or belief.

Schiller felt that his expression made a more persuasive argument by "substituting the coldly logical and less ambiguous 'right to postulate' for the more inflammatory 'will to believe,' and by explaining that neither phrase commits us to anything but a recognition of the activity and enterprise which underlie and actuate our knowing." [45]

In Schiller's philosophy, knowing is possible because problems are provocative to a purposive organism. There is no such thing as a disinterested search for the truth—even among the philosophic brotherhood. He wrote: "Philosophers in their inquiries are not often animated, even in their own minds, by the disinterested love of truth they advocate. For more commonly they are trying to prove some pet theory of their own, in a more or less surreptitious manner." [46]

Philosophers or non-philosophers, we come at our problems with a subjective bias. We have an interest. We are anything but a *tabula rasa*. "All our actual knowing is selective. It always clears its way through a jungle, by selecting a part from a larger whole, cutting out the superfluous, rejecting the rubbish." [47] Somehow, according to Schiller, the logician has never quite come face to face with the psychological aspect of knowing. This they leave out in order to achieve their so-called objectivity of meaning. "Every postulate has a psychological origin. It comes into being because it has commended itself to its maker's mind, and issues from his total personality." [48]

One of the persistent questions in philosophy is: what is the real? And one of the persistent answers to this question is: that which is objective; the real is prior to and independent of the knower. Schiller did not accept this answer, but held that we make our own reals. He said: "The most real object we acknowledge had first to be made an object of thought by our selection. No fact is fact till it is taken as a fact." [49] Truth is not something that forces its way upon us; we look for it. "For we cannot afford to remain unresistantly passive, to be impressed, like the tabula rasa in the traditional fiction, by an independent external world which stamps itself upon us. If we did that we should be stamped out." [50] He said that we look for the relevant. "To say that relevance means subjectivity merely means that it is conceived not as a quality residing in the thing thought per se but only in its relation to us." [51] Schiller passed us this challenge: "It requires some perspicacity to perceive that the fact which is really a fact is always a value." [52]

Some, we have noted, seek their objectivity in logic. But there, Schiller found personality. "Logic cannot transcend the limits of personality." [53]

Others hope to achieve objectivity through science and its advances in instrumentation. Again, Schiller said no. "Actually all scientific data and observations are in the first instance personal affairs. They arise from the personal observations of those who attest them." [54] And the nature of knowing is not much changed by new instrumentation.

> But instruments do not fundamentally alter the problem of knowledge. They do not absolutely guarantee either exactness or immunity from error. Thus (a) while it is true that the more exact we make our instruments the more minute grow the quantities they enable us to measure, yet the more numerous also grow the sources of error we must guard against, because to a fine measurement errors become relevant which are not appreciable in a

rough one. . . . (b) Every instrument has limits to its
exactness. . . . (c) When we want an accurate observation we have soon to recognize that the conditions are so
complex and so variable that anything may upset
them. . . . (d) However fine we make our instruments
and however carefully we observe and correct our observations, we come sooner or later to a point at which we rely
once more on the observer's sense. For he has to read off
the record of his instruments.[55]

Once more, we find that we cannot escape from ourselves, even
though the introduction of ever more complicated devices en-
courages us to think that we have done so. Schiller believed it
was high time that "some one challenged the facile assumption
that personality must always be a source of error and failure in
our knowing." [56] He thought it was high time that someone
pointed out the misnomer of the term "pure science." "What is
so called should be conceived as a late and extreme specializa-
tion of the impulse-to-know which has grown very remote from
the immediate urgencies of action." [57]

Many of the quotations from Schiller have been taken from
his early works. All of them seem consistent with the following
passage from his last book.

The natural starting point for all humanist metaphysics
will be, of course, the great saying of Protagoras, which is
the first statement of humanism, and one of the deepest of
philosophic dicta. Man is the measure of all things; of
things that are that they are, of things that are not that
they are not. No completer statement of relativity is conceivable; it plainly anticipates Einstein by its reference to
the problem of measurement, but it enunciates a more
thorough-going relativity than any physics has as yet
found use for.

It serves as a salutary reminder that every problem, every belief, every reality, every truth is relative to man the knower, and that it is meaningless to trouble about unknowable "reals." This, however, in no wise denies that there may be reals as yet unknown to us, which we may sometime know; it merely assures us that when that day comes they will come into relation with our minds. It removes, therefore, all apprehension that our life may be doomed to failure, because essentially dependent on what does not exist for us, and it warns us against vain speculation about reals unrelated to us. The real world which concerns us, which we should seek to measure, conquer, and control, is one related to us and necessarily relative to our apprehension, and this is the best and most hopeful feature about it. It is not unknowable and inaccessible to human thought and unresponsive to its operations. The real world is *our* real world, measurable by *our* standards. . . . Surely there is nothing in this doctrine which is anything other than an encouragement to thought.[58]

Dewey did not care much for so highly subjective and highly personalistic an approach. He never went as far in that direction as did James and Schiller. But it may be safe to say that the progression of Dewey's thought over his long life tended toward that direction. His de-Hegelization ran from actional to interactional to transactional, and at the transactional he was getting a little closer to the positions that had been taken by James and Schiller. Peirce was never near these positions at all. He remained essentially an analytical philosopher from beginning to end.

From *Essays in Experimental Logic,* 1916, to *Knowing and the Known,* his last publication, 1949, Dewey faced the problem of subjectivity. In the earlier book he wrote:

The thesis of the essay is that thinking is instrumental to a control of the environment, a control effected through acts which would not be undertaken without prior resolution of a complex situation into assured elements and an accompanying projection of possibilities. . . .

Such an instrumentalism seems to analytic realism but a variant of idealism. For it asserts that processes of reflective inquiry play a part in shaping the objects. . . . In so far as it is idealistic to hold that objects of knowledge in their capacity of distinctive objects of knowledge are determined by intelligence, it is idealistic.[59]

This is the "ego-centric predicament." There is an "interaction of an organism with other things." [60] "Sense data differ from individual to individual." [61] The following is anticipatory of his later transactionalism: " . . . Different positions or different internal structures . . . introduce differences in the phenomena which they respectively have a share in producing. . . ." [62]

Dewey as an interactionist held the view that persons and things interact, and out of these interactions we get our picture of reality. In *Knowing and the Known*, he discarded the interactionist point of view for the transactional. The difference is spelled out thus:

We name these three levels . . . Self-Action, Interaction, and Transaction. These are all human behaviors in and with respect to the world. . . .

Self-action: where things are viewed as acting under their own powers.

Inter-action: where thing is balanced against thing in causal interconnection.

Trans-action: where systems of description and naming are employed to deal with aspects and phases of action, without final attribution to "elements" or other presumptively detachable or independent "entities," "essences," or "realities," and without isolation of presumptively detachable "relations" from such detachable "elements." [63]

The wording is not very helpful, but it gives us some notion of the change that was taking place. The following may be more helpful.

A "real world" that has no knower to know it, has, so far as human inquiry is concerned (and this is all that concerns us), just about the same "reality" that has the palace that in Xanadu Kubla Khan decreed. . . . A knower without anything to know has perhaps even less claim to reality than that. It does not deny the geologic and cosmic world prior to the evolution of man within it. It accepts such a world as known to us, as within knowledge, and as with all the conditionings of knowledge; but it does not accept it as something superior to all the knowledge there is of it. [64]

It may be seen that knowings and knowns have become "twin aspects of common fact." Dewey now viewed transaction as "The knowing-known taken as one process in which in older discussions the knowings and the knowns are separated and viewed as in interaction." [65] Dewey arrived at a new definition of reality.

Reality: As commonly used, it may rank as the most metaphysical of all words in the most obnoxious sense of metaphysics, since it is supposed to name something which lies underneath and behind all knowing, and yet, as Reality, something incapable of being known in fact and as fact.[66]

Dewey indicated reality was to be sought in the transaction occurring between the observed and the observer rather than in either side exclusive of the other.

The term "transaction" that Dewey originated in his last publication was to become the name for a psychology based on the perception demonstrations of Dr. Adelbert Ames, Jr. Geiger said that "transaction became a key symbol in Dewey's final work." [67] Geiger held that some of this position had been present in Dewey for many years. But there is a difference, and Dewey made this difference clear in his Foreword to Earl C. Kelley's *Education for What Is Real.* "In the following pages Professor Kelley has restated at the outset some educational principles and standards that have been urged upon teachers more or less in the last half century. . . . But none of them had the force of out-and-out demonstration." [68] Demonstration was precisely what Ames did. After him there was a more empirical basis, a more experimental basis, for the subjectivism that we have been discussing as it occurs in the writings of James, of Dewey to some extent, and especially of Schiller.

From some of the writings by persons close to the Ames perception demonstrations we may obtain a better statement of transaction psychology than Dewey gave us. These authors have used expressions paralleling those of Schiller. Franklin P. Kilpatrick, closely associated with the work of Ames from the start, acknowledged that the "possibility of reducing observations to absolute objectivity is basic to much of our thinking," and that it "underlies most theorizing concerning the nature of science," [69] but stated that the work of Ames in his perception demonstrations pointed away from this conclusion. Ames's work, he said, "suggests strongly that the search for absolute objectivity is a vain one. Apparently, the correspondence between percept and concept is never absolute." The closest possible approximation of correspondence Kilpatrick called "functional probabilities." [70]

When one considers that Schiller's comments were largely directed toward discrediting certain philosophical ideas and that Kilpatrick's comments concerned demonstrations first conducted by Dr. Ames at Hanover, New Hampshire, in the 1940's, one can be impressed by the similarity of statement.

> Man never can know more of the external world than those aspects which are directly relevant to the carrying out of his purposes. Each man's perceptions are therefore his own, unique and personal; common perceptions become possible in so far as common experiences and common strivings are shared among individuals. This approach places perceiving squarely within the context of human striving, the "thing perceived" being inseparably a part of the "process of perceiving" and both reflecting "reality," only by virtue of the active participation of the perceiver in the full-bodied, on-going process of living.[71]

While these demonstrations were new, the conclusions drawn from them were theories that had been developed in the past without the benefit of demonstrations. Kilpatrick found the philosophies of James, Dewey, and Whitehead supportive. Dewey, as we have seen, lived long enough and was discerning enough to be a part of the group that gave the original impetus to transactional psychology. C. J. Herrick, a distinguished neurologist, was another who thought along the lines of the transactionalists. He observed:

> The bias which arises from unrecognized personal attitudes, interests, and pre-conceptions is the most treacher-

ous of all the subversive enemies of sound scientific progress; yet these attitudes and interests are the key factors in
all really original scientific investigation. This issue must
be faced frankly and courageously. The easy way out is to
ignore the troublesome personal ingredients of the problem and say that science has no concern with them. This
is now generally regarded as the standard, or normal,
scientific method. But actually this cannot be done, and
we cannot afford to try to do it; for the interests and
attitudes of the inquirer shape the whole course of the
investigation, without which it is meaningless and fruit-
less. To neglect these components of scientific work and
the satisfactions of a successful outcome is to sterilize not
only the process but also the results of the inquiry.[72]

Hadley Cantril, who has apparently been as close to the
work of Ames as anyone and has perhaps written as much as
anyone about transactional psychology, has used phrases
strongly suggestive of some of Schiller's. For example:
"Whether any scientist likes to admit it or not, any interpretation he makes must be regarded as a value-judgment." [73] According to Cantril, we could use a new definition of objectivity: " . . . Our knowledge of perception, showing that 'the
nature of reality' as we experience it would not exist *except* for
the assumptive world we bring to a concrete situation, flatly
contradicts the contention that the scientist can be objective in
any such sense." [74] By that he meant in the sense that reality is
external to the knower.

A more recent statement by Cantril carried equally Schillerian terminology. "According to our view, all aspects of the
environment, whether they are physical or social, exist for us
only insofar as they are related to our purposes. If you leave out
human significance, you leave out all constancy, all repeatabil-
ity, all form." [75] The world, as we experience it, "has no

meaning and cannot be defined independent of the experience." [76] The proper place to begin our studies is with the perceiving individual.

It seems strange that transactional psychology and transactional philosophy have not had a better press in educational philosophy and in educational psychology. Beyond the books by Earl C. Kelley of Wayne University and the work of a few others, there has not been a very effective exposition in the literature of education. Geiger's summary is probably as good an abridgment as there is: " . . . Experience is in fact the result of an active co-operation between knower and known," [77] and " . . . knowledge is a matter of vital participation in a world of which it is a part rather than the idle glances of a disinterested and outside watcher." [78] Here is Geiger's listing of the essential aspects of transactionalism:

> The following items may indicate quickly how a naturalistic and necessarily relativistic theory of knowledge will have consequences differing sharply from those entailed by a static spectator theory:
>
> (a) knowledge can be neither discovery nor disclosure of an aloof and already predetermined existence, for the very nature of knowing depends upon a *joint* achievement of organism and environment;
>
> (b) so, the knower, as well as the perceived environment, is part of his knowledge;
>
> (c) individual differences in knowledge among men can be detected and controlled, eliminated or prized; but the general human element in all knowledge can be neither isolated nor eliminated;
>
> (d) scientific knowledge is relative to knowers in specific contexts;

(e) thus, what something may be when totally independent of any observer or frame of reference is a scien-
tifically meaningless question, for knowledge is a
transaction.[79]

Geiger warned, "We have been slipping from a theory of
knowledge to one of value. This has not been inadvertent. The
two concepts must join." [80]

Without objectivity, without this anchorage in an independent reality, everything is permitted. Without it, we are on our
way to a "cosmic impiety." Actually, we should rework Russell's and Lippmann's fears into a new way of looking at
subjectivity. The case against the realization of pure objectivity
has been stated over and over, but over and over we have been
urged to seek objectivity at all costs. A more sensible approach
would suggest that we come to terms with a subjectivity that
seems inevitable. We seem to have preferred, however, to go
right on preaching objectivity rather than accepting subjectivity and working out a new operating procedure.

Nietzsche anticipated this problem. To him, objectivity did
not mean "disinterested contemplation (which is a rank absurdity)," but rather, knowing "how to put the most diverse
perspectives and psychological interpretations at the service of
intellection." [81]

Let us, from now on, be on our guard against the hallowed
philosophers' myth of a "pure, will-less, painless, timeless
knower"; let us beware of the tentacles of such contradic-
tory notions as "pure reason," "absolute knowledge," "absolute intelligence." All these concepts presuppose an eye
such as no living human being can imagine, an eye required to have no direction, to abrogate its active and
interpretative powers—precisely those powers that alone
make of seeing, seeing *something*. All seeing is essentially

perspective, and so is all knowing. The more emotions we allow to speak in a given matter, the more different eyes we can put on in order to view a given spectacle, the more complete will be our conception of it, the greater our "objectivity." But to eliminate the will, to suspend the emotions altogether, provided it could be done—surely this would be to castrate the intellect, would it not? [82]

This could be James, but for the different style of writing.

We have been so persuaded to rule out the emotions that until recently we would hardly imagine that emotions could help us to a more adequate perception of something. Nietzsche's point is strongly contemporary: as we permit the emotions to get into the act, we increase the number of eyes by which we perceive the scene. To the cold eye of science we add the warm eye of art, and we increase the vision.

Eric Dardel said that we have recently been freed from "the superstition of objectivity." Since we are all "guilty" of subjectivity, there is one sure thing we can do. "The best way of exercising subjectivity wherever it might degenerate into arbitrariness or fantasy, the only true opposition to subjectivism, is not to deny its role in a work of science but to be aware of it." [83]

Abraham Kaplan approached the problem somewhat more methodologically with this view: " . . . Either values must be rigorously excluded from science, or else they must themselves be given an objective ground. It is this second alternative which seems to me methodically sounder. For I do not see how values can be excluded." [84] The problem in scientific methodology is "not whether values are involved in inquiry, but . . . how they are to be empirically grounded." [85] Kaplan implied that we should make a scientific study of values so that we could more effectively weigh the part values play in our speculations and observations. This procedure would not eliminate values, but it would tend to "ground" them empirically, thus minimizing the arbitrariness and fantasy that Dardel mentioned. Kaplan restated objectivity as "intersubjectivity." The "intersubjectivity becomes the mark of objectivity, for it testifies that the observation is uncontaminated by any other factors save those common to all observers." [86] Although not all the details of Kaplan's approach have been worked out, his ideas are suggestive of productive research. Too often the objectivist refuses to apply his scientific skills to a careful study of the impingement of value on science.

Ross L. Mooney, a student of transaction and creativity, has taken the position that we fail to study the experimenter himself. We look at the researched and overlook the researcher, in our haste to achieve objectivity. This is a product of habitually viewing science as "revealed out there" rather than "created in here." [87] He said, "The important operations which have to do with the development of self-understanding and self-discipline in the regions of participation and observation are given very little attention." [88] The primary concern of the research man should be "the study of the nature of his own inquiry."

> The data are not inherent in the objects in the situation, taken as separated from him, but are inherent in his experience as formed within operations involving himself and those objects. In studying rocks, for example, a scientist can report that a rock is red, is heavy, dissolves in chemical X, burns when placed in fire, and so on. The data of redness, heaviness, dissolution, and burning are perceptions within his experience, not apart from it.[89]

The person who would become a scientist should "accept himself as involved in all he does." He should be aware of his participation and not afraid and apologetic for the "intrusion of any subjectivity." In this context subjectivity is not some intrusion of human imperfectibility but the "primary instrument for scientific enterprises." [90] Science is grounded in "a field of beliefs." He emphasized: "It is easy to forget this fact. In our effort to establish findings 'beyond doubt,' we are prone to wish we were men 'beyond beliefs.' " This inclination, Mooney said, can lead to "loss of perspective" and "lack of humility." [91] His views sound quite contrary to Russell's allegation of "cosmic impiety."

Since we cannot get away from ourselves, since we cannot separate knowings from knowns and observers from observed, we would improve our situation if we cherished our subjectivity instead of decrying it. An honest subjectivity would seem to advance the cause of science, or any other cause, better than a false and impossible objectivity.

In addition to the moral value of honesty, there is another moral advantage. For too long, scientists, under the banner of objectivity, have denied responsibility for their deeds. Scientists have brought forth their discoveries and then left them like orphans on the church steps. This creates indifference to the social consequences of scientific advances. Science "is detached because detachment is thought to be the strength and security of academic method," Baker Brownell has declared. "It is amoral because it fears the contamination of concerns for things beyond the limits of its own special problem." He called this "the purity of withdrawal." [92] Lewis Mumford has made an attack on the impersonal attitude among scientists. He said, "The ideal of scientific thought was to be as free from personal bias as if it were the product of a machine." Cold, detached, rigorous, unemotional, objective—all these are considered laudatory by the scientist when applied to him. Mumford called this an "abdication of responsibility" and a cause of "the resurgence of barbarism." [93] Mumford and Joseph Wood Krutch seemed at times to be hell-bent on damning scientists without making an equivalent effort to show how they might incorporate science and themselves in a transactional relationship. The enemy is not the scientist; it is a concept of objectivity.

James, Dewey, and Schiller did not see any insoluble conflict between subjectivism (or personalism, we may say, in regard to James and Schiller) and the scientific method. The two can go hand in hand; indeed, they have to go hand in hand. In this context, Schiller's philosophy seems most relevant. He saw that if man is the measure of all things, then man cannot escape the responsibility of his own acts. Man cannot assign his responsibility to a public philosophy based on natural law, or to an externality independent of mankind, or to some transcendent entity. As Camus has suggested, only the future is transcendent.[94] We do the measuring and we do the acting.

If, under subjectivism, everything is possible, then our need is to develop selves equal to this possibility. With Schiller: "An honest man will always try to say what he means." [95]

1. Albert Camus, *The Myth of Sisyphus* (New York: Vintage Books, 1959), p. 35.

2. Walter Lippmann, *The Public Philosophy* (New York: New American Library, 1956), p. 132.

3. *Ibid.*, p. 133. There is reason to suppose that men can no longer accept this rather naïve discussion of subjectivity and objectivity since the appearance of Michael Polanyi's *Personal Knowledge* (University of Chicago Press, 1958). It is interesting to note that Huston Smith in the seventh John Dewey Society Lecture, "Condemned to Meaning," 1965, and A. H. Maslow in the eighth John Dewey Society Lecture, "The Psychology of Science," 1966, made references to Polanyi's work. Another dimension of this discussion may be found in Floyd W. Matson, *The Broken Image* (New York: Doubleday & Co., 1966).

4. *Ibid.*, p. 134.

5. *Ibid.*, p. 134.

6. *Ibid.*, p. 136.

7. P. W. Bridgman, *The Way Things Are* (Cambridge: Harvard University Press, 1959), p. 6.

8. P. W. Bridgman, *The Logic of Modern Physics* (New York: Macmillan Co., 1960 [paper back]), pp. x–xi.

9. Bridgman, *The Way Things Are,* p. 2.

10. *Ibid.*, p. 56.

11. *The Education of Henry Adams,* p. 447.

12. Frederick S. Breed, "Education and the Realistic Outlook," in N. B. Henry (ed.), *Philosophies of Education* (Chicago: University of Chicago Press, 1942), p. 101.

13. *A History of Western Philosophy,* pp. 827–88. Copyright © 1945 by Bertrand Russell. It is interesting to note that Walter Lippmann uses this same quotation in *The Public Philosophy,* p. 135.

14. William Earle, "Notes on the Death of Culture," in Stein, Vidich, and White (eds.), *Identity and Anxiety* (Glencoe, Ill.: Free Press, 1960), pp. 369–76.

15. Charles Sanders Peirce, *Collected Papers* (Cambridge: Harvard University Press, 1958), VIII, 189.

16. *Ibid.*, VIII, 182.

17. *Ibid.*, V, 336.

18. *Studies in Humanism,* p. 20.

19. Schiller, *Riddles of the Sphinx,* p. 160.

20. *Our Human Truths,* p. 176.

21. *Riddles of the Sphinx,* p. vii.

22. *Ibid.*, p. 142.

23. *Studies in Humanism,* p. 18

24. *Our Human Truths,* p. 178

25. *Ibid.*, pp. 178–79.

26. *Humanism,* p. 45.

27. *Ibid.*, pp. 44–45.

28. *Studies in Humanism,* p. 182.

29. *Ibid.*, pp. 182–83.

30. *Riddles of the Sphinx,* p. 261.

31. *Ibid.*, p. 133.

32. *Studies in Humanism*, p. 243.

33. *Ibid.*, p. 432.

34. *Riddles of the Sphinx*, p. 134.

35. *Studies in Humanism*, p. 198.

36. *Ibid.*, p. 55.

37. *Our Human Truths*, pp. 98–99.

38. *Ibid.*, p. 171.

39. *Ibid.*, pp. 8–9.

40. Paul Weiss, "Pragmatists and Pragmatists," review of *Logic for Use*, in *New Republic*, March 26, 1930, p. 161.

41. Schiller, *Logic for Use*, p. 374.

42. *Our Human Truths*, p. 292.

43. Schiller, "Axioms as Postulates," in Henry Sturt (ed.), *Personal Idealism* (London: Macmillan Co., 1902), p. 70.

44. *Ibid.*, p. 91.

45. *Logic for Use*, p. 340

46. *Ibid.*, p. 13.

47. *Ibid.*, p. 314.

48. *Ibid.*, p. 340.

49. *Ibid.*, p. 449.

50. "Axioms as Postulates," p. 55.

51. *Logic for Use*, p. 77.

52. *Ibid.*, p. 37.

53. *Ibid.*, p. 351.

54. *Our Human Truths*, p. 90.

55. *Logic for Use*, pp. 370–71.

56. *Our Human Truths*, p. 9.

57. *Ibid.*, pp. 191–92.

58. *Ibid.*, pp. 181–82.

59. John Dewey, *Essays in Experimental Logic* (New York: Dover Publications, n.d.), p. 30.

60. *Ibid.*, p. 410.

61. *Ibid.*, p. 411.

62. *Ibid.*

63. John Dewey and Arthur F. Bentley, *Knowing and the Known* (Boston: Beacon Press, 1960), pp. 107–8.

64. *Ibid.*, p. 136.

65. *Ibid.*, p. 304.

66. *Ibid.*, p. 300.

67. George R. Geiger, *John Dewey in Perspective,* p. 16.

68. John Dewey, Foreword, in Earl C. Kelley, *Education for What Is Real* (New York: Harper & Bros., 1947), p. v.

69. Franklin P. Kilpatrick, "Statement of Theory," in Franklin P. Kilpatrick (ed.), *Human Behavior from the Transactional Point of View* (Hanover, N.H.: Institute for Associated Research, 1952), p. 87.

70. Kilpatrick, *ibid.*, p. 88.

71. *Ibid.*

72. Quoted by Hadley Cantril *et al.*, "Psychology and Scientific Research," *ibid.*, p. 209.

73. *Ibid.*, p. 208.

74. *Ibid.*, pp. 208–9.

75. Hadley Cantril, "A Transactional Inquiry Concerning Mind," in Jordan M. Scher (ed.), *Theories of the Mind* (New York: Free Press, 1962), p. 338.

76. *Ibid.*, p. 387.

77. George R. Geiger, "An Experimentalist Approach to Education," in Nelson B. Henry (ed.), *Modern Philosophies and Education* (Chicago: University of Chicago Press, 1955), p. 140.

78. *Ibid.*, p. 141.

79. *Ibid.*

80. *Ibid.*

81. Friedrich Nietzsche, *The Birth of Tragedy and the Genealogy of Morals* (New York: Doubleday & Co., 1956), p. 255.

82. *Ibid.*, pp. 255–56.

83. Eric Dardel, "History and Our Times," in *Identity and Anxiety*, p. 586.

84. Abraham Kaplan, *The Conduct of Inquiry* (San Francisco: Chandler Publishing Co., 1964), p. 387.

85. *Ibid.*, p. 387.

86. *Ibid.*, p. 128.

87. Ross L. Mooney, "Problems in the Development of Research Men," *Educational Research Bulletin*, September 12, 1951, p. 145.

88. *Ibid.*, p. 145.

89. *Ibid.*, p. 141.

90. *Ibid.*, p. 142.

91. Ross L. Mooney, "Groundwork for Creative Research," *American Psychologist*, September, 1954, p. 544.

92. Baker Brownell, *The College and the Community* (New York: Harper & Bros., 1952), p. 55.

93. Lewis Mumford, *In the Name of Sanity* (New York: Harcourt, Brace & Co., 1954), p. 194 ff. Also note Joseph Wood Krutch, *The Measure of Man*, 1954.

94. Albert Camus, *The Rebel* (New York: Vintage Books, 1958), p. 166.

95. *Logic for Use*, p. 65.

VI. The Return to Dialogue

Academic philosophy appears to approach what Whitehead called "the restraint of serious thought within a groove . . . ," where "a development of particular abstractions, and a serious contraction of concrete appreciation" divorces the mind "from the concrete contemplation of complete facts." [1]

Philosophy is peculiarly adapted to sequestration in a groove, for it has so often found shelter in closed systems and anti-systems. Schiller described an encounter between two philosophers thus: "They take their stand firmly on their dignity and never emerge from the protective shadow of their 'systems.' Each speaks pontifically in his own language." Within his own system and language each finds safety in "obscurity, technicality, and the invention of a new terminology." His opponent is left in the uncomfortable predicament of being unable to confute what he does not understand. "So the creator of a new branch of 'learning,' pseudo-science, or metaphysics can easily pose as the hierophant of ineffable mysteries and enjoys practically complete immunity from attack." [2]

But this immunity from attack proves to be rather illusory.

The Aristophanesean "cloud cuckoo town" is a precarious philosophic paradise. The philosopher becomes "terribly worried by all the other philosophers, each of whom is as cantankerous and cranky as himself, and wants to carry him off to his own private Nephelococcygia. . . . They all get very angry," observed Schiller. "They get so angry that they cannot even laugh at each other."[3] And so they end up by just gibbering at each other.

Systems are, of course, a necessary part of philosophy. Whitehead said, "We must be systematic; but we should keep our systems open."[4] And now a closed-system attitude seems to threaten educational thinkers with restraint within a groove. In the process of systematizing an admittedly ever loose discipline, some seem to be more interested in shooting down a fellow from the protective shadows of their own systems than in trying to understand him within the reference points of his system.

Schiller criticized the Oxford of his day:

> . . . Oxford, which has organized itself as an asylum for lost causes, skillfully cultivates, by means of its classical and historical studies, a backward-looking bias in its alumni. The true 'Greats' man is meant to go down indelibly imbued with the conviction that in matters of importance nothing has been discovered or said since Plato and Aristotle, and that nothing else matters.[5]

However, his disenchantment was by no means confined to Oxford. He generalized that "no one familiar with the actual working of academic institutions is likely to fall into the error of pinning his faith to them."[6]

Schiller was not one to hide his philosophic displeasure under a technically erudite vocabulary. Nor was he one to take on second-generation disciples when he could have a go at the prophet himself. What is more, he struck out against the central concern of a philosopher and not at some obscure detail. He called Aristotelian logic a word game, a handy device for whipping generations of schoolboys at examination time, and a trick for working one's opponent into a corner rather than a careful pursuit of truth. Schiller was also critical of the Cartesian method of doubt: "But Descartes was too much the pupil of the Jesuits to see any but the bad side of doubt. His methodical doubt was not conceived as a method of exploration, but as a device for anchoring himself to an impregnable rock of certainty as speedily as possible." [7]

In Kant, it is the Categorical Imperative that annoyed Schiller.

> Kant's Categorical Imperative claims to be the supreme law of Duty, the sum and substance of morality. But, practically, it is null and void. It has no content. Nothing is deductible from it. . . . Whatever action is taken in any case can be universalized with perfect impunity. For in its complete uniqueness it never recurs; so we can formally affirm that what we did was right, and should be done in all cases, knowing full well that there can never be another such case.[8]

To Schiller, the Categorical Imperative was "impotent to guide action in any way. It shouts, 'Do your duty!' but refuses to tell us what our duty is, or how we may distinguish right from wrong." [9]

As for the ethical theory expounded by his contemporaries, Schiller comments:

> Theoretical ethics is a broken reed. No intelligent man can live long in any academic atmosphere without becom-

ing aware that academic ethics has no positive moral
value. Indeed, on the whole its value is strongly negative.
It is often positively demoralizing. The academic disputes
as to how (if at all) the Good is to be defined, and how it
is related to pleasure, may conceivably be a good mental
gymnastic, though even this may be doubted. . . .

Morals, they [professors of morals] say, merely provide
the material for ethical theories to contemplate and specu-
late about, and it is vulgar and Philistine to look for any
more intimate and vital relation between theory and practice. Substantially the same answer is given to a second
objection that ethics, as it is taught in universities, diverts
our natural moral energy into unprofitable channels, and
fritters it away in the futile discussion of artificial and
antiquated subtleties which never mattered much and have
long ceased to have any practical meaning, while it leaves
aside untouched and unmentioned, the real pressing problems of moral life.

This second charge leads to a third, the most damaging
of all. Moral philosophy is practically useless, not merely
because it has adopted a false theory of the relation of
theory to practice. Its professors have intentionally, of
malice prepense, and in their own selfish interests, made it
useless and meaningless, in order to shirk a theoretic
problem which they could not solve and dared not to
touch, lest it should get them personally in trouble. This
problem concerned the application of moral principles to
concrete cases. . . . So, in order that the purity of moral
principles might run no risks of contamination from contact with the solid facts of life, they proceeded to make
them inapplicable in principle.

The culmination of this sort of trickery—for it is nothing more—is to be found in the Categorical Imperative of
Kant, which ostensibly proclaims the sacrosanctity of Duty
with tedious reiteration, while actually forbidding us

what, in fact, our duties are. It is still esteemed in academic circles as the supreme effort and example of a pure morality, and largely accounts for their emptiness. Its academic admirers have overlooked the damning fact that it is only "safe" because it is utterly meaningless. For a principle that cannot be applied to concrete cases at all, or can be made to answer them in any way one pleases, is as meaningless and worthless in theory as it is in practice.[10]

Schiller was suspicious of both mathematics and exactitude. He said, "Any use or application of a mathematical 'truth' is always precarious." [11]

It is amazing what a spell the ideal of exactness has cast upon the philosophic mind. For hundreds, nay thousands, of years philosophers seem to have been yearning for exactness and hoping that, if only they can attain it, all their troubles will be over, that all the pitfalls in the way of philosophic progress will be circumvented and that every philosophic science, from psychology and logic to the remotest heights of metaphysics, will become accessible to the meanest understanding.[12]

But for all their professions of concern for exactness, philosophers have been most careless about bringing exactness to their practice. Indeed, they are strangely reluctant to define just what they mean by exactness. Schiller remarked, "Apparently they are content to refer to mathematics as an 'exact' science and to admonish philosophy to respect and aspire to the mathematical ideal." [13]

But, as Schiller saw it, so great an appeal to mathematics leaves philosophy in a position of subservience that is not altogether reassuring.

> At Cambridge philosophy is not thought to aim at an independence of the sciences . . . but it seems to lapse into the opposite extreme of subservience to the sciences. It emulates science and aspires to the "exactness" of the abstruser aspects of mathematics. By rivalling them in technicality it hopes to raise itself to an equality of scientific rank and so to escape accusations of being a pseudo-science. It remains, however, difficult to say how philosophy differs from science, what additions it can make, and why it should be needed in the first place. For the analysis on which it prides itself seems to be a wholly verbal and ephemeral thing, liable to be superseded at any moment by the discoveries of the sciences.[14]

Schiller saw, perhaps unfairly, the goal of analysis as the fixation of meanings. Ayer has said that philosophy is the provision of "Definitions *in use,*" and that it is not the task of philosophy to provide definitions in a dictionary sense.[15] One wonders whether a philosophy that even takes "definitions in use" as its major contribution might still contribute to what Schiller called an "endeavor to arrest the natural growth of meanings which attends the growth of konwledge." [16]

> We must let our words develop with our knowledge and power.
> We cannot, therefore, base genuine and fruitful predictions on the present meanings of our words. For we cannot foresee what changes they may have to undergo. . . . The pretensions of the formal logician to foresee the future and predict it without fail by "analysing" the present meaning of our words is fantastic and absurd. It is "wishful thinking" which measures nothing but the height of his presumption and the depth of his ignorance and conceit.[17]

Schiller felt that the growth of philosophic analysis had given us "bombastic technicality and impenetrable obscurity," which made "the most formidable chapters of Whitehead and Russell . . . seem simple, easy, popular and unscientific." [18]

In the final paragraph of his last book, Schiller said:

> I am driven to the conclusion that logistics is an intellectual game. It is a game of make-believe, which mathematically trained pedants love to play, but which does not on this account become incumbent on every one. It may have the advantage that it keeps logisticians out of other mischief. But I fail to see that it has either any serious significance for understanding scientific knowledge or any educational importance for sharpening wits.[19]

Under its spell, "philosophers shrink from their big and thrilling problems and confine themselves to a number of technical questions about which they can discourse harmlessly and endlessly with a show of erudition." [20]

It was a ready willingness in James, Dewey, Mead, Schiller, and sometimes in Peirce, to treat big and thrilling problems that gave early pragmatism both a warmth and a vigor that is all too often missing in philosophy. Engagement and confrontation were as basic to pragmatism in its origins as its new way of looking at truth.

A tragic aspect of pragmatism in this decade of the twentieth century is the disappearance of some basic dimensions that it had when it first came into view. Some of its original inspirations have died. The result has been a loss of dialogue with various other schools of philosophy and a loss of dialogue with its own earlier spirit. It has been suggested here that a first step in getting at this original spirit would be the reading of

Schiller. The reason for beginning with Schiller is not that he was a better man or a better philosopher than James or Dewey or Mead. We would turn to Schiller precisely because he is relatively unknown. There are merits in this circumstance. Schiller is not buried beneath commentary and commentary on commentary. People have not made up their minds about him; they have pretty well constructed their philosophical niches for James and Dewey. Schiller's niche in the 1960's is scarcely more than an urn holding forgotten ceremonial ashes.

Pragmatism, especially as it was applied to education, developed a few non-Whiteheadean grooves between 1910 and 1960. For a good number of those years, pragmatism, particularly in educational philosophy, became John Dewey. Despite his modesty, Dewey acquired a following of loyal disciples. Mead, at best, had a mere handful, and his failure to write books left this handful without a scripture to quote. No biblical *Democracy and Education* for the followers of Mead. In attracting bands of faithful disciples, James enjoyed greater success as a psychologist and somewhat less success as a philoso-proselytes. In a sense, Peirce is still in the process of being rediscovered.

Dewey was the main part of pragmatism. On this point, there can be little dispute. But he was not the whole of pragmatism. In some ways he is the most "dated" of the founders of American pragmatism. George Geiger wrote that Dewey's "mood of healthy-mindedness . . . perhaps more than anything else . . . tends to date Dewey." [21] Healthy-mindedness could be an appropriate philosophical dimension for an America with a Western frontier or even for an America that went out to save the world for democracy. But with Hitler and the Nazis piled atop Freud and Marx, Dewey's healthy-mindedness could no longer satisfy man's craving for a philosophical treatment of agony, despair, absurdity. As Geiger has reminded us, we find no sense of anxiety or loneliness or anguish in Dewey; nor do we meet with existential torment and frustration in the pages of his works.[22] It would not have occurred to Dewey to define education as Kierkegaard did: "What is education? I should suppose that education was the curriculum one had to run through in order to catch up with oneself, and he who will not pass through this curriculum is helped very little by the fact that he was born in the most enlightened age." [23] Nor would Dewey have used such titles as *Fear and Trembling* and *The Sickness Unto Death*. Perhaps Dewey was too unmindful of his contemporary, Freud.

Although Dewey was one of the most broadly concerned and involved philosophers of the modern era, there were lacunae in his scope that prevented him from being the complete philosopher for our day. Pragmatism suffered as an educational philosophy by operating too exclusively as Deweyism.

If excessive healthy-mindedness was a Deweyist groove, another groove, which developed through no fault of Dewey, was the obsession of educational pragmatists in the 1930's with method. Monotonously and faithfully, students wrote in their notebooks in course after course, year after year, such phrases as "the scientific method," "the democratic process," "the method of reflection," and so on. Theodore Brameld's criticism may have been a little harsh, but one must admit its relevance. Brameld found an overemphasis on experimental methodology as "the key to progress," with interest centered upon "process rather than product." He commented, "Like the American culture of which it is an ideological ally, it has been much more concerned to delineate an effective methodology of intelligent practice than to formulate the goals for which that methodology is indispensable." [24] During the 1930's some professors so exhausted themselves discussing the principles of academic freedom that they had no energy left to say anything worthwhile in demonstration of the principles they espoused. Process and product have to be related; there were those who never got beyond talking about process or method. Somewhere along the line, these educational philosophers misplaced or missed what Dewey had to say about means and ends. For a time educational philosophers with a pragmatic orientation were trapped in a methodological groove.

But more serious than the grooves were the failures of dialogue. There was a failure of dialogue with European philosophy. Granted that the Germans and the British could scarcely bring themselves to see philosophic efforts in the United States as anything more than a pipsqueak challenge to the European establishment as headquarters of philosophy in the West. Analytic philosophy landed on our shores in some part as the result of the Hitlerian Diaspora. Pragmatists were slow to recognize the new arrival, although the work of Moore and Russell was contemporaneous with much of the ascent of pragmatism in American philosophy.

As pragmatism became increasingly the preserve of the educational philosopher and the progressive educator, there followed a failure of dialogue with academic philosophy. A polarization occurred on many university campuses, dividing the departments of education from the departments of philosophy. There were exceptions, to be sure, but the very eagerness with which communication is sought today is an index of the previous separation.

Another dialogic failure separated pragmatism as an educational philosophy from the humanities. Arthur Bestor's metaphor of an iron curtain dividing the educationist from his liberal arts colleague is exaggerated, but one would be the victim of academic myopia if one denied the isolationism that became evident in American higher education. Jacques Barzun, Bernard Bell, and Arthur Bestor were, perhaps, engaged in promoting self-fulfilling prophecies; but withal, their observation had basis in fact.

Pragmatism, especially in the Chicago environment, had come to life as a phase of the general liberal or progressive movement in America, around the turn of the century. Here flourished the social thought that revolted against an older philosophical and political formalism. The leaders of the movement were John Dewey, Thorstein Veblen, Justice Oliver Wendell Holmes, Charles and Mary Beard, James Harvey Robinson, Jane Addams, Horace Kallen, George Herbert Mead, and other familiar names. For a while it had the New School for Social Research as one of its bases of operation.

The University of Chicago was the original base. Less important centers were scattered about the land. But gradually the leaders died or were retired. Eventually pragmatism suffered its failure to remain in dialogue with political liberalism and the ranks of labor. The dialogue, which began in Chicago, tapered off in New York. The focus grew narrower; the adherent became more cautious. The main currents trickled into nostalgia.

A further failure was the dialogue with religion. The pragmatists rested their oars after Dewey wrote in *A Common Faith* about "the distinction between 'religion' as a noun substantive and 'religious' as adjectival." [25] The book was published in 1934, and since that date, the pragmatists have been content to engage in periodic warfare with religion and theology. We have reason to believe this warfare is coming to a close; or in any case, the older battle strategies have grown quite obsolete. Dialogue is possible.

As Mead reminded us, "the continued reconstruction of the world goes on—reconstruction not only of the future but of the past. . . . We are continually reconstructing the world from our standpoint." [26] So perhaps we need to reconstruct pragma-

tism from the vantage point of an era conditioned by Sartre and
Wittgenstein. The present review of pragmatism largely
through an examination of F. C. S. Schiller suggests the following as essential dimensions of reintegrating pristine pragmatism: *a*) science as a central avenue for understanding man in
his individual-social context and for the solution of his problems in whatever arena; *b*) pluralism as opposed to monism; *c*)
subjectivism, which takes the position that we cannot escape
wholly from ourselves however hard we may try; *d*) social
reformism, which is especially associated with John Dewey; [27]
e) analysis, which is especially associated with C. S. Peirce,
but which is by no means absent from James, Dewey, or
Schiller; *f*) personalism—or voluntarism—which we may call
existentialism without abusing any of these terms to excess,
found most clearly in James and Schiller; *g*) a concern for
man as a religious being, with James and Schiller as obvious
representatives of this aspect.

Some may object that the above itemization is merely a
facile inclusion designed to make pragmatism all things to all
men. The response to this possible objection is: Read the
pragmatist statements published before 1910, and watch out
for the restrictions placed on pragmatism since 1910. This is
not to suggest that pragmatism as it existed prior to 1910 is the
answer to all of man's troubles some fifty or sixty years later.
Rather, it is to suggest that if we will approach our problems
with the breadth of early pragmatism supplemented by the
somewhat narrower emphases of contemporary analysis and
existentialism, we may escape from some of the unpleasant
dichotomies and consequent acrimony that characterize present
educational philosophy. Pragmatism is today anything but a
moribund philosophy. Many elements that are being heralded
today as philosophical frontier efforts can be found in early
American pragmatism.

For all that has happened since 1910, the early pragmatic statements regarding science retain peculiar relevance. Reuben Abel, in a paper read in honor of Schiller's centennial year, defended pragmatism as being that philosophy which is especially helpful in a world dominated by science. Pragmatism grows more timely rather than less so.

> . . . A philosophy may during its career experience an era of resurgence and renewed vitality. Some new interest, some insoluble practical problem, some nagging human difficulty, perhaps some empirical discovery (Darwin? Freud? Pavlov? Einstein?) may result in making a specific philosophy particularly insightful, or appropriate, or revealing, or adequate, or enlightening, or persuasive, or whatever it is that promotes adherence to a philosophy.
>
> It is in this sense that I think pragmatism is peculiarly fitted to meet the philosophic needs of the Twentieth Century, and, in particular, to be the philosophic foundation for some of the knowledge obtained, and some of the problems posed, by the outlook of modern science. It is this latter which I wish to document.[28]

Abel presented nine points to support "the unique pertinence of pragmatism to the characteristic outlook and problems of the world of modern science." [29] Abel made this summation:

> In its theory of reality as constituted by the interaction of man and his environment, and its view of truth as entailing human activity and inquiry, the philosophy of pragmatism provides a framework for understanding the concepts, constructs, facts, theories, and laws of the sciences; for comprehending the status of geometry and logic; for dealing with such problems as determinism, induction,

probability, and rationality; for a theory of meaning; for
the procedure of the historian; and for an attitude of
empiricist open mindedness which may well be the most
enduring contribution of philosophy to the human enterprise.[30]

Even if one questions whether Abel supported his thesis as
fully as he claimed, one would have a hard time giving any
other philosophical formulation the support Abel gave to pragmatism as a philosophy of science.

Few persons have so delighted in pluralism as James and
Schiller. Our delight may have been diluted by our fear of
atomism, a stigma word in our day. But pluralism as a philosophical position is an equivalent to the exploratory quality in
science. It is openness to new experience. It suggests that the
future may be different; the die has not been finally cast.

Paul Goodman has long complained of the lack of variety in
education. He has held that "throughout our educational system" we have a "desperate need for institutional variety." [31]
David Riesman has voiced regret that Americans, whether they
are thinking about international affairs or about personal matters, suffer from an inadequate formulation of their alternatives.[32] C. Wright Mills has said that the study of history is
carried on to show us alternatives.

We study history to discern the alternatives within which
human reason and human freedom can now make
history. . . . Freedom is not merely the chance to do as
one pleases; neither is it merely the opportunity to choose
between set alternatives. Freedom is, first of all, the
chance to formulate the available choices, to argue over
them—and then, the opportunity to choose. . . . The so-

cial task of reason is to formulate choices, to enlarge the
scope of human decisions in the making of history. . . .
The future is what is to be decided. . . .[33]

And here is Robert Ulich's answer to those who would see
pluralism merely as a more attractive name for atomism: "Only
that world society could be really fruitful and uniting that
would be pluralistic in the sense that it would appreciate rather
than fear differences. Yet such a pluralistic society would not
be atomistic, as our world of today may sometimes appear to
the critical spectator." [34] Our diversified world would escape
from atomism by a central respect for human dignity. There
would be love, truth, and justice.

In our present situation, educators are in dire need of some
philosophical encouragement to accept pluralism. It is refreshing
to come upon this in Schiller: "A plethora of truths is not the
same as none at all." [35] Again: "The oldest thing, perhaps,
about philosophy and science alike, is how little attention they
have paid to the alternatives to accepted views, even when
these alternatives were logically obvious and inherently quite
as probable as the accepted views." [36]

Atomism suggests isolation; pluralism suggests freedom and
the search for new forms of relationships.

Over the years all manner of philosophers and theologians
have joined forces to make man feel guilty about beginning his
philosophizing with himself. To begin with himself was hu-
bristic. For some reason, man was supposed to find some person, or force, or site, beyond himself; only thus could he display
the proper humility before the great mystery, whatever that
great mystery might be. While man has been exhorted to divest
himself of his own intimate subjectivity, it has never been
made clear how he should go about it. Furthermore, a certain

vagueness has hovered over that objectivity that he was to find so irresistible and so immutable.

Man starts with himself. How else? Schiller said:

> All scientific phenomena are relative to the human faculties by which they are apprehended and known. Neither colours nor temperatures could exist for totally colour-blind percipients devoid of temperature sense; nor would logical contradictions irk a mind that was not painfully affected by them. In fact, sense perceptions and logical necessities are just as relative to man as are the values, which are usually admitted to depend on human valuations. Hence, there is no getting away from the old dictum of Protagoras: man is the measure of all things; and to man are referred all the things he knows or can know.[37]

Starting with himself does not compel man to end there. It can lead quite readily to Dewey's concept of democracy as "the widening of the area of shared concern." It can lead to Ulich's concept of "cosmic reverence," by which he meant "not only a person's respect and love for other persons or for a cherished idea or institution, but for a sense of the belongingness of all created things to a common ground of life." [38] This common ground could be called God, or Father, or Nature, or Cosmos. Ulich also spoke of "self-transcendence," the encouragement of man to "realize his potentialities by participating in ever-widening circles of experience and responsibility." He emphasized, "The main criterion is that man be understood as a being that always can go further, reach out, and climb above himself." [39]

Bertrand Russell wrote:

> Philosophy, throughout its history, has consisted of two parts inharmoniously blended: on the one hand a theory

as to the nature of the world, on the other an ethical or political doctrine as to the best way of living. The failure to separate these two with sufficient clarity has been a source of much confused thinking. Philosophers, from Plato to William James, have allowed their opinions as to the constitution of the universe to be influenced by the desire for edification: knowing, as they supposed, what beliefs would make men virtuous, they have invented arguments, often very sophisticated, to prove that these beliefs are true. For my part I reprobate this kind of bias, both on moral and on intellectual grounds. Morally, a philosopher who uses his professional competence for anything except a disinterested search for truth is guilty of a kind of treachery. . . .

Intellectually, the effect of mistaken moral considerations upon philosophy has been to impede progress to an extraordinary extent.[40]

Whatever may have been the ill effects of moral considerations upon philosophy qua philosophy, there can be no question that in educational philosophy, whatever the intrinsic merits of analysis or the contributions it may make to elucidation and clarity, analysis cannot be an adequate response to the full range of problems with which our schools deal. Harry Broudy has commented:

Nearly everyone is agreed that our language needs cleaning up, but in educational philosophy, as in general philosophy, agreement as to what we ought to mean when we say something is still far from substantial.

If one asks for an educational appraisal of this elucidation, my answer must be that substantively the results have not been impressive, but if I were to hazard an explanation, it would go something like this: Too many of the problems in education are not due to misuse of language or logical carelessness. Too often conflicts over curriculum, teacher training, institutional arrangements arise and persist because the parties to the quarrel understand each other's language only too well. The current controversies about professional education may exemplify horrible misuses of language and deplorable lapses of logic, but fundamentally these are value conflicts, not linguistic problems.[41]

No one can be so naïve as to imagine that with linguistic cleansing all controversy would subside. The notion that educational conflicts are in essence linguistic may grind progress to a complete halt.

Education is already largely a government responsibility, and most evidence suggests that the public representatives of society will increasingly manage education. But further and more importantly in the present context, we may assume that education will increasingly be the method for changing and reforming society. If we accept Whitehead's definition of civilization as the progressive substitution of persuasion for force, then, realizing the dangers inherent in modern weapons, we must look to education as the method of maintaining civilization. There was a time when one could fairly accuse education of engaging in empire-building, of trying to enlarge its field of operation. This accusation is scarcely applicable today. Now society sends its problems to the schools rather than the schools seeking out new areas to dominate. Just about every social problem eventually comes to roost in the classroom. One has only to think of the war on poverty to realize this trend. Jencks said that "inadequate as schools and colleges may be to meet the non-academic responsibilities thrust upon them, the fact that America has turned to educators for help testifies to the failure of other institutions to do what is necessary." [42] This is another expression of Dewey's early description of the school as a residual institution. Such a residual institution as the school cannot turn its back on society, cannot pride itself on finding its philosophy in a value-free posture and a pretense of non-commitment. As Frederick C. Neff put it, Dewey and Bode "did not apologize for gearing education to a continuous realization of the free way of life, and the clarity with which they spelled out their goals remains unsurpassed." [43] Lewis S. Feuer concluded an essay on Dewey and the back-to-the-people movement with these words:

> Our age finds it hard to understand Dewey and even harder to sympathize with him. In philosophy, ours is an age of narcissism. We are in a trough in the cyclical history of the human conscience, and the "do-gooding" motives of Dewey, Jane Addams, and Beard seem hollow and naive to the proponents of managerial philosophy. Perhaps the repressive outlines of the technicians' universe will be challenged once more, however, by a more wholly human vision. [44]

In 1897 Dewey wrote: "Education is the fundamental method of social progress and reform." To decry the dimension of social reform in pragmatism is to invite a position of irresponsibility and irrelevance.

Because education is in the public domain, it is subject to constant pressures from the political and educational slogan-makers. It is therefore necessary to have slogan-analyzers. It is also necessary to have careful writing, since educational theorizing brings together a multitude of disciplines and research projects. The folk expression, "Everybody went to school, therefore everyone is an authority on education," has its counterparts in the field of educational philosophy where this kind of superficial specialism leads to the allegation that educational philosophy is a philosophical slum. "But it need not be so," R. S. Peters has written. "There are genuine and exciting philosophical problems in this field. Indeed, there is enough work to keep a company of trained philosophers busy for half a century." [45]

Israel Scheffler has seen the analysts as helping to "stimulate the application of newer philosophical approaches to education." Analysis is not "a panacea for the practical difficulties attending the schooling of the young." But it can contribute to "improving our *understanding* of education by a clarification of our conceptual apparatus." [46] There is enough work and enough kinds of work in education that no one need be turned away.

The syndrome of healthy-minded confidence and humorless social emphasis in Deweyean pragmatism made it as inappropriate as is today's educational technician's approach for dealing with the anxious existential man in the contemporary world. At home, we are trying to bring the disadvantaged into the mainstream of American life. Beyond our shores, we are trying to help millions of Asians and Africans in their efforts to move from an agricultural to an industrial civilization. The simple solution of making everyone in the United States into a member of the middle class and everyone in the world into an admiring cog of industrialism would be just too simple. M. I. Berger has written that education "today lacks passion because it ignores the existence of man, *qua* man." [47] Man can be flattened out by our productive system. This is the thesis adopted by Herbert Marcuse in *One Dimensional Man*. "In this society, the productive apparatus tends to become totalitarian to the extent to which it determines not only the socially needed occupations, skills, and attitudes, but also individual needs and aspirations." [48] Its sweeping rationality becomes itself irrational.

Also, there is some reason to believe that one may be flattened out by the educational apparatus. This is the continuing theme in the books and articles by Paul Goodman. This is the basis for the many protests taking place on college campuses. Dostoevsky held that the whole purpose of a man's life is to prove that he is not a piano key. To Jason Epstein, the danger at the high-school level is that education will flatten students into acting as "functionaries in an enveloping technocracy rather than as individuals in the private pursuit of unsuspected truths." [49]

The hard core of existentialism (or to use a term more correct historically in the present context, personalism) in James and Schiller was buried beneath indifference to personalism by those who thought themselves followers of John Dewey. Mead, who displayed a lifelong concern for the self, actually belonged with Dewey, according to Paul E. Pfuetze. Pfuetze concluded that Mead was a social behaviorist and Buber an existentialist. "William James would have understood Buber better than his younger pragmatist brother Mead." [50] One may add that Schiller, too, would have understood Buber better.

In renewing acquaintance with the existentialist content in the work of James and Schiller, we can, in effect, update pragmatism. We restore a dimension that was largely overlooked for several decades. Henry David Aiken commented:

But we no longer have the fine old confidence of Dewey's middle period that if we simply stick to the method of science, or intelligence, all will be well. I at least am just a little envious of Dewey in this regard. But my envy also marks the limits of his use to me.[51]

What is missing in Dewey may be found in James and Schiller. There is a genuine stream of existentialism in their philosophies. This dimension once more suggests that pragmatism remains a timely philosophy when viewed in its originating state. "The self has hitherto been nothing but one of the great and conspicuous failures of philosophy," Schiller said.[52] He emphasized, "It will not do for any philosophy to ignore personality." [53]

The existentialist content and concern in James and Schiller largely account for their continuing dialogue with religion. James was not engaging in mere tender-minded generosity when he observed that "pragmatism may be a happy harmonizer of empiricist ways of thinking with the more religious demands of human beings." [54] To him, pragmatism widened "the field of search for God." He explained:

> Rationalism sticks to logic and the empyrean. Empiricism sticks to the external senses. Pragmatism is willing to take anything, to follow either logic or the senses and to count the humblest and most personal experiences. She will count mystical experiences if they have practical consequences. She will take a God who lives in the very dirt of private fact—if that should seem a likely place to find him.[55]

This was not affectation. This was the pluralistic openness we find in both James and Schiller.

The thesis of this book is that a review of pragmatism gives us these dimensions: an adequacy for understanding and guid-

ing the contemporary advances in sciences; a pluralism in keeping with the demands of society and personal identity; a subjectivism that affords as radical an anchorage in objectivity as
can be found; a social reformism that is an inevitable part of any
relevant philosophy; a persisting analytic emphasis; a personalist
character that is anticipatory of current existentialism rather
than antithetical; and finally, a concern for religion. Each of
these dimensions, in one way or another, opens the way for the
restoration or deepening of dialogue with significant movements
in modern life. Together they offer a counterforce to the failures
of dialogue that have occurred. Together they suggest that the
dialogue may be enlarged to include the alienated lonely within
the Western world and the stranger without. Within, there is a
frightening summons for dialogue, and beyond, an even more
frightening summons for dialogue beckons. Pragmatism *with*
Schiller lends a sense of hope that those dialogues will take
place.

While the dimensions of early pragmatism foreshadow a
rather complete philosophy, much important work remains to
be done. This is an advantage, for the doom of a complete
philosophy is stagnation and death.

1. Alfred North Whitehead, *Science and the Modern World*
(New York: New American Library, 1948), pp. 196–97.

2. *Our Human Truths*, p. 101.

3. Schiller, *Humanism*, pp. 266–67.

4. Whitehead, *Modes of Thought*, p. 8.

5. F. C. S. Schiller, *Tantalus* (London: Kegan Paul, Trench,
Trubner, 1924), pp. 33–34.

6. *Ibid.*, p. 28.

7. *Problems of Belief*, p. 20.

8. *Ibid.*, pp. 137–38.

9. *Ibid.*, p. 138.

10. *Social Decay and Eugenical Reform*, pp. 32–34.

11. Schiller, *Problems of Belief*, p. 24.

12. Schiller, *Our Human Truths*, p. 338.

13. *Ibid.*

14. *Ibid.*, p. 82.

15. Alfred Jules Ayer, *Language, Truth and Logic* (New York: Dover Publications, 1946), p. 59.

16. *Our Human Truths*, p. 336. See also John E. Smith, *The Spirit of American Philosophy* (New York: Oxford University Press, 1963), chap. vi.

17. *Our Human Truths*, pp. 336–37.

18. *Ibid.*, p. 317.

19. *Ibid.*, pp. 344–45.

20. *Ibid.*, p. 101.

21. *John Dewey in Perspective*, p. 160.

22. See above, p. 43.

23. Soren Kierkegaard, *Fear and Trembling* and *The Sickness unto Death* (New York: Doubleday & Co., 1954), p. 57.

24. Theodore Brameld, *Education for the Emerging Age* (New York: Harper & Row, 1965), pp. 32–34.

25. P. 9.

26. George Herbert Mead, *Movements of Thought in the Nineteenth Century* (Chicago: University of Chicago Press, 1936), p. 417.

27. C. Wright Mills would include William James as social reformer. James was active in the anti-imperalism movement of the past century. See C. Wright Mills, *Sociology and Pragmatism* (New York: Paine-Whiteman Publishers, 1964), chap. xiv.

28. Reuben Abel, "Pragmatism and the Outlook of Modern Science," *Proceedings, New England Philosophy of Education Society* (Bridgeport, Conn.: University of Bridgeport, 1964), pp. 9–10.

29. *Ibid.*, p. 22.

30. *Ibid.*

31. Paul Goodman, *Compulsory Mis-education* (New York: Horizon Press, 1964), p. 154.

32. David Riesman, *Abundance for What?* (Garden City: Doubleday & Co., 1964), p. 40.

33. C. Wright Mills, *The Sociological Imagination*, p. 174.

34. Robert Ulich, *Philosophy of Education* (New York: American Book Co., 1961), p. 146.

35. *Our Human Truths*, p. 184.

36. *Ibid.*, p. 168.

37. *Ibid.*, pp. 96–97.

38. Ulich, *op. cit.*, p. 121.

39. *Ibid.*, p. 88.

40. *A History of Western Philosophy*, pp. 834–35. Copyright © 1945 by Bertrand Russell.

41. Harry S. Broudy, "The Role of Analysis in Educational Philosophy," *Educational Theory*, October, 1964, pp. 267–68.

42. Christopher Jencks, "Cultivating Greater Diversity," *New Republic*, November 7, 1964, p. 33.

43. Frederick C. Neff, "Let Them Eat Cake," *Educational Forum*, May, 1964, p. 406.

44. Lewis S. Feuer, "John Dewey and the Back to the People Movement," *Journal of the History of Ideas*, October–December, 1959, p. 568.

45. R. S. Peters, "Comments," in John Walton and James L. Kuethe (eds.), *The Discipline of Education* (Madison: University of Wisconsin Press, 1963), p. 20.

46. Israel Scheffler, *Philosophy and Education* (Boston: Allyn & Bacon, 1958), pp. 1–3.

47. M. I. Berger, "Existential Criticism in Educational Theory," *School and Society*, November 11, 1964, p. 335.

48. Herbert Marcuse, *One Dimensional Man* (Boston: Beacon Press [paperback ed.], 1966), p. xv.

49. Jason Epstein, review of *New Curricula*, *New York Review of Books*, December 31, 1964, p. 15.

50. *Self, Society, Existence*, p. 231.

51. Henry David Aiken, "Revaluations: John Dewey's Darwinism," *New York Review of Books*, April 22, 1965, p. 18.

52. *Our Human Truths,* p. 10.

53. *Ibid.,* p. 8.

54. William James, *Pragmatism and Other Essays* (New York: Washington Square Press, 1963), p. 33.

55. *Ibid.,* p. 38.

Index

Index